BORN INTHE FIRE

CASE STUDIES IN CHRISTIAN ETHICS AND GLOBALIZATION

ENOCH H. OGLESBY

THE PILGRIM PRESS
NEW YORK

Biblical quotations, unless otherwise noted, are from the Revised
Standard Version of the Bible, copyright 1946, 1952, © 1971, 1973 by the
Division of Christian Education of the National Council of the Churches
of Christ in the U.S.A., and are used by permission.

Book design by Publishers' WorkGroup
Cover design by Jim Gerhard

Library of Congress Cataloging-in-Publication Data

Oglesby, Enoch H. (Enoch Hammond)
Born in the fire : case studies in Christian ethics and
globalization / Enoch H. Oglesby.
p.   cm.
Includes bibliographical references.
ISBN 0-8298-0849-3
1. Christian ethics. 2. Black theology. 3. Liberation theology.
4. Africa, Sub-Saharan—Religion. 5. Afro-Americans—Religion.
I. Title. II. Title: Globalization.
BJ1251.044   1990
241'.08996—dc20   90-43875
CIP

The Pilgrim Press, 475 Riverside Drive, New York, NY 10115

To the memory of V. H. Oglesby,
Mother in the struggle,
Whose faith was truly
Born in the fire.

To the memory of G. B. Perkins,
Who sowed the seeds
Of education and hope
In the minds and hearts
Of the world's children.

For Charles and Gaby Hein
For Peter K. Njoroge
For Gloria P. Oglesby
Still faithfully walking among us,
Whose passion for freedom and life
Continue to inspire hope in the
God of all creation.

CONTENTS

CONTENTS

Introduction

In my own African pilgrimage, my parents' and grandparents' deep faith—hewed largely from the mountains of despair and hope in America's South—has been renewed. Their nurturing faith in the liberating promise of the gospel of Jesus Christ became a connecting link, as I experienced firsthand the beauty and paradox of African peoples and cultures during a sabbatical year in Kenya, East Africa. As an African-American middle-class theologian, it is existentially difficult if not impossible, except by the grace of God, for me to eliminate all of the negative misconceptions, illusions, deceptions, and misbeliefs that are associated with the term "African" in the public culture of Western society.

If it is true that language both shapes and reflects reality, then it is reasonable to assume that ethically sensitive people must try out a "new language," which then becomes an alternative conceptual lens with which to "see" the "African" and to critique their own worldview. For example, unmasking and dismantling the Hollywood image of the African as portrayed in movies such as *Tarzan* must be part of a permanent moral struggle. A scandal to conscience and an affront to human dignity, such movies have often depicted the African as mindless, savage, uncivilized, and forever dependent on the white European for guidance and social affirmation. Such negative images and racial stereotypes tug at one's conscience. Nevertheless, these misconceptions have been played out and reinforced over centuries of betrayal, neglect, and colonialism.

These prevailing "images" of historical oppression, suffering, and pain notwithstanding, I experienced a liberating African hospitality as I learned from and shared in African culture at the grassroots level of community life. In terms of the broader struggle for justice, peace, and liberation, the surprise of my sabbatical year was my discovery that "the blood that unites us as brothers and sisters in the global village is thicker than the waters that divide us." We are a pilgrim people. We are a people of hope. We are a people still in formation—shaped continuously by the wind and fire of God's love and grace—as we live between the dialectical poles of brokenness and wholeness, experience and expectation. In the religious idiom of the black church in America, "God ain't finished with us yet!" As a pilgrim people, ours is a faith born in the fire.

This book is an outgrowth of my sabbatical experience. In terms of Christian ethics, I try to provide a useful forum for dialogue on the moral issues of faith and cultural diversity, identity and suffering, power and morality, and the struggle for liberation and wholeness in the global community. I hope also to make here a modest contribution to the theological discussion on the importance of faith stories as a catalyst for human liberation for those with a shared memory of oppression.

The initial impetus for this project was an experiment in the use of the case study method that involved in-depth interviews with indigenous people from African countries, East Africa and Kenya in particular, about their religious experiences, sufferings, and hope for the future. I collected and analyzed these conversations in case form and compared them with the life stories and values of American blacks whose lives have been shaped by the impact of Christianity in the modern world.

While many moral issues, problems, and concerns emerge in the context of individual case studies, in this book I focus on the dynamics of faith and liberation in intercultural and crosscultural context. These are dominant motifs not only in black church life in America but also in what is commonly known as "African theology" and in the cultural life of the global community. At the practical level, I have developed ten case studies from an African context and ten from the perspective of American black religious experience. It has been said that a person's spiritual journey actually mirrors various stages of that individual's liberation and personal moral growth. If there is any truth to this claim, then we will find the stages of growth as well as a liberating spirituality reflected in the life experiences of ordinary people.

The cases in this book reflect a contemporary mosaic of human experiences on critical issues ranging from education, adultery, and AIDS to problems of loneliness, guilt, sexism, and oppression in our global community. They discuss crosscultural and pastoral issues ranging from grassroots politics to polygamy, from the tensions of traditional authority in African society to the crisis of the black family and economic survival in American society. Perhaps the unifying thread in these diverse case experiences is the presence of an uncommon faith in the God of compassion and justice. This unitive thread of faith holds together the fragments in which struggling and marginal people live. No people can fully live without faith. Hence, these diverse stories of faith are actually born in the fire of hope that can burn down all barriers of oppression in the global community.

At the theological level, I believe that storytelling, that is, a narrative perspective, helps us to clarify the issues at stake in liberation and faith in the African-American context. All communities of faith—whether they are concerned with liberation from oppression or with maintaining the status quo—require a narrative that enables them to know and remember their own struggles as a people of God. In human community, storytelling, with its own peculiar power to shape identity, teaches us about social reality, about suffering and joy, and about despair and hope in ways abstract reasoning or theological speculation can not.

In Part 1 of this book I provide a comparative conceptual framework for understanding the themes of faith and liberation in terms of globalization, ethical clarity, storytelling, and the ways in which we are shaped by folk proverbs and religious values. For African people, storytelling has been a dominant tradition for transmitting values, religious beliefs, morals, rituals, and customs from one generation to another. I focus particular attention in this volume on the importance, in both African and African-American communities, of folk proverbs in shaping social character relative to the themes of faith and liberation.

Part 2 comprises twenty case studies. The cases out of the African religio-cultural context are placed first. Whenever possible, I have given critical attention to thematic development.

One cannot do serious theology, even less ethics, in the abstract. Only in the throes of real life situations can fundamental questions of theology, pastoral care, and ethics be raised. To help the reader, at the end of each case is a discussion note and questions that serve as a model for reflection and dialogue.

I wish to acknowledge and thank the Association of Theological Schools for a generous full-year grant to do research and travel abroad, especially in the countries of eastern Africa. I further wish to thank many of my faithful colleagues, friends, and students, who gave me the benefit of constructive dialogue and encouragement along the way in the completion of this project—particularly Allen Miller, Charles Hein, Jacob C.

Oglesby, Peter K. Njoroge, Fred Gomendo, Mother Crummie, and Lowell Zuck, to name only a few. My deep thanks as well to my editor, Stephanie Egnotovich, and the rest of the staff at Pilgrim Press for their assistance and ethical sensitivity. I am also indebted to my typist, Kay Boyle at Eden Theological Seminary, who rendered invaluable assistance in the final stages of the manuscript.

Finally, a special word of appreciation and love must go to my wife, Gloria, who labored untiringly with me at the Institute for Ecumenical and Cultural Research—especially on the earlier drafts of the manuscript. She remains today, perhaps, my best constructive critic.

1

ETHICAL
FOUNDATIONS

A spider's web united can tie up a lion.
                                    —*African proverb*

We will go before God to be judged,
and God will ask us, "Where are your wounds?"
And we will say, "We have no wounds."
And God will ask, "Was nothing worth fighting for?"
                                    —*Rev. Allan Boesak*
                                    South Africa

1
GLOBALIZATION
ETHICS

There is neither Jew nor Greek,
There is neither slave nor free,
There is neither male nor female;
For you are all one in Christ Jesus.
(Gal. 3:28)

Many ethically sensitive people feel that, as we attempt to live a life of faithfulness in the world, there is a critical need for "global awareness" within the family, the church, the seminary community, and the nation. Yoshiro Ishida, director of the Center for Global Mission at the Lutheran School of Theology at Chicago, argues for a global perspective in our institutions. Ishida says, "Globalization is a matter of the educating power of particular human relationships across cultural lines. . . . Concrete human presence and awareness of the worldwide human community must contribute a new 'air' to a school if its educative effects are to be global."[1] Ishida underscores here the importance of globalization at both the cognitive and affective levels of Christian witness in human life.

I believe that the church is called to be the light of the world and the salt of the earth; it is called to be a bridge over the troubled waters of racism, sexism, classism, militarism—and all the other demonic "isms" in our world that divide the body of Christ. In the words of Martin Luther King, Jr., the church must be a "headlight" rather than a "taillight" for the global community; it must be a prophetic magnet or "love force" that has the capacity to draw people and nations of diverse cultures together. The church is the reconciling agent throughout the *oikoumene*, the whole

3

inhabited earth. The church is called into being by God, through the revelation of Jesus Christ, for the sake of the *oikoumene*.[2]

This means that the gospel of Jesus Christ is good news in the *oikoumene* precisely because of God's love for us while we were yet sinners. For Christians, there is unity in humanity because of what God did for us in the person and works of Jesus Christ. Therefore, any viable notion of globalization must resist the temptations of cultural myopia, dogmatism, moralism, and theological provincialism. The new reality of globalization, despite its conceptual ambiguity, can, in fact, give the church alternative ways of perceiving and experiencing the faith and love of God.

There are four elemental and interrelated issues that must be understood before one can successfully do globalization ethics: (1) a functional definition of globalization ethics; (2) preconditions to doing globalization ethics; (3) ethical norms and contexts of globalization in the life and faith of the church; and (4) the importance of the case study method for understanding globalization ethics.

WHAT IS GLOBALIZATION ETHICS?

In today's ecumenical and multicultural communities, we often hear many of the church's scholars and leaders speak of "globalization." Many images come to mind when we think about the concept of "globalization ethics." In the ecumenical community of faith, the idea of globalization ethics is powerful precisely because it conjures up conflicting images. For some, combining the words "globalization" and "ethics" means breaking with dominant Western intellectual and theological traditions in search—both existentially and socially—of a national culture free from the pains of colonialism.[3] For others who are disillusioned with the promises of capitalism and economic prosperity, the idea of globalization may provide a convenient escape from the despair, violence, and narcissism of a material culture. Still others may see it simply as another trend or faddish phenomenon in the perennial quest for cosmic truth and meaning beyond the historical ambiguities of time and space.

Regardless of the various ways Christians interpret globalization ethics, its significance is not lessened. For it challenges us to grapple with the problems and moral dilemmas of the Christian faith in a world of religious and cultural diversity.[4] The willingness to risk the vulnerability of trans-contextual dialogue is an identifying mark of doing globalization ethics. We can see or experience the world differently only as we are culturally

4

dislodged and repositioned in relationship to the reality of the gospel of Jesus Christ.

What, then, is globalization ethics? Globalization ethics is not oriented toward conventional morality, which is based on blind loyalty to traditional creeds and church dogma. Rather, it is based on the revelation of Jesus Christ as the new paradigm for the moral life. Globalization ethics has its own distinctive norms and sources. Its integrative norm is Jesus Christ as Liberator and Reconciler in our broken world. The normative source of globalization ethics is Jesus Christ and the revolutionary claims of the gospel to set the oppressed free for right living, faithfulness, love, and the experience of the new community as children of God.

John C. Bennett argues in *The Radical Imperative* that in order for morally sensitive persons in the global community to read the Bible accurately, they must recognize Christ as the center and norm.[5] Indeed, Bennett implies and I agree that women and men in the contemporary church must have new charts on which to study "globalization issues" of justice and liberation and how we may better interrelate theology and social ethics.[6] Because the gospel is revolutionary, Jesus as normative paradigm challenges us to change oppressive structures in our global village and to resist the seduction of the status quo and the accompanying tendency to group people into a condescending social stratum of "us" and "them." Of Jesus' ethical teachings, Bennett observes, "Jesus turns upside down the world's and the conventional churches' classifications of people."[7]

The roots of globalization ethics in the reality of the gospel has enormous implications for case studies of faith and liberation. One of the clues essential to understanding globalization is found in Jesus' own address in the synagogue in Nazareth:

> The Spirit of the Lord is upon me
> because [the Lord] has anointed me to preach good news to the poor.
> [The Lord] has sent me to proclaim release to the captives
> and recovering of sight to the blind,
> to set at liberty those who are oppressed,
> to proclaim the acceptable year of the Lord.
>
> (Luke 4:18–19)

As the norm and center for moral life, Jesus Christ is the real source of authority in our understanding of globalization ethics. Scripture teaches us that he entered a broken and troubled world to do a new thing, to establish a new pattern for the moral life in the global community. On the practical level, Jesus Christ came into the world to "set the captives free." The profound moral insight behind Jesus' message is that we are set free not only by words but also by deeds. Therefore, globalization ethics is a self-critical attempt to *walk* our *talk*. Our language of faith, justice, and compassion must be mirrored through the doing of our being in God. Because of who God is, Jesus Christ and his ethical teachings become the "new pattern" for the moral life in the global community.

The new pattern is marked by radical freedom and the love of God and neighbor. In short, the global model of community is this: Such a community—whose center is Jesus Christ—lives under the total rulership of the Holy Spirit. Such a community is an instrumentality of justice and peace in the world. Such a community is a sign of healing and wholeness in the midst of cultural fragmentation and brokenness. Such a community practices a self-giving love whose impetus moves the church beyond the discord and conflicting interests of race, class, gender, and national loyalties.

Both the prophetic vision and the moral dilemma of globalization ethics can be seen in a poignant observation made by Donald Shriver on the challenge of theological education in the global church:

> Theological education must speak and act towards the building of the visible unity of the church in the broken world. In a time when the disunity of the human race as a whole threatens the very existence of the race, the disunity of the churches is as great a disservice to the world as it is a scandalous denial of God's love for the world.[8]

The church must always be about the tasks of mission and of speaking a word of hope and unity in the midst of our brokenness. To a people of faith, doing globalization ethics is a self-critical way of addressing the meaning of brokenness, suffering, and alienation in our world. The process of globalization ethics affirms, therefore, the principles and values inherent in the gospel as a way to speak the "truth to power" and to speak the "truth-in-love." The former is implied in Shriver's notion of forces that lead to disunity as a "scandalous denial of God's love for the world"; the latter refers to the redemptive power of *agapeistic* love to build a "visible unity of the church in the broken world." Here the ultimate logic or rationale for the presence of a "globalization ethic" is not simply the threat of the mutual annihilation of nations and races, but, more importantly, God's passion and love for the world that we all may be saved by the blood of Jesus Christ. For example, the gospel of John is explicit concerning God's love for the world and suffering humanity:

For God so loved the world that [God] gave [God's] only Son, that whoever believes in him should not perish but have eternal life. For God sent the Son into the world, not to condemn the world, but that the world might be saved through him. (John 3:16–17)

PRECONDITIONS OF DOING
GLOBALIZATION ETHICS

The term "precondition" refers to that which is necessary in order for us to better understand the nature of globalization ethics. I also mean to suggest by its use a way of thinking that engages the mind and heart in a life of moral discourse on the important issues of human community. For example, each person has an obligation to be morally serious about issues of faith and freedom. In this sense, using the term precondition is a way of suggesting provisional guidelines for interpreting life and death issues in the global community. It invites us to be clear even about the definition and discourse of ethics itself.

Before we can understand the dynamics of moral reasoning and faith, we must define the term "ethics." Charles L. Kammer, in *Ethics and Liberation*, provides a helpful definition. Quoting from Arthur J. Dycke, he asserts, "In a very general way, ethics can be defined as systematic reflection upon human actions, institutions, and character."[9] Kammer raises a central ethical question, What should we be as persons? and emphasizes the importance of "character" in dealing with the issues of oppression and liberation in our world. At every level of life—individual, communal, or global—ethics must perform the critical function of discerning "the sort of persons we ought to be" in the light of what we are called to do as children of God. For Christians, therefore, ethics must prod our conscience over the question of "character," or our essential being in community.[10]

Accordingly, the first of the preconditions necessary for doing globalization ethics is the cultivation of Christian humility. Genuine humility is a sobering virtue the world over. Given the egocentrism prevalent among Christians in the West, it is easy to understand why the gospel of Jesus Christ speaks a harsh word against the sins of pride and self-exaltation: "For every one who exalts himself will be humbled, and he who humbles himself will be exalted" (Luke 14:11).

Perhaps both the logic and irony of globalization ethics lie in its invitation and challenge to middle-class Christians of the First World, in particular, to learn how to sit with the poor, the least and last, in the "low places" of our world community. Indeed, Kammer suggests such a global vision, one that is capable of revealing a deeper truth of the mystery of our own existence. He emphatically proclaims:

> There is no room in the world for Christian arrogance or the assumption by any group that it, and it alone, is in full possession of the truths of existence. Life remains a mystery whose origins and purposes remain hidden. Christians do have some glimpses into these mysteries, insights they share with others. But, the history of Christian peoples, marked by brutality and insensitivity to others, shows that there is much we do not understand. We must be open to the insights that others bring and collectively probe the mystery of our existence.[11]

A second precondition for doing globalization ethics is recognizing the importance of the case method in studying the issues of faith and liberation with respect to the lives of individuals in human community. As we shall see later, the case method is a way for us to dialogue, to agonize over, and to respond to the problems and moral dilemmas of human life in the light of a freeing and unfailing God. Dialogue is enormously relevant to marginalized people who live at the edges of existence.

A third precondition for doing globalization ethics—especially in regard to Christian witness—is a *confessional* mode of faith wherein the giver and receiver listen to and share in each other's stories. What we confess or say to each other can shape the way we perceive and experience the world. For example, the Christian who readily affirms, "I believe in justice" or "I believe in the love of God" can influence another's fundamental life orientation. What can I believe? A litany of confession may read:

> O God, I am so fragile:
>   my dreams get broken,
>   my relationships get broken,
>   my heart gets broken,
>   my body gets broken.
> What can I believe,
>   except what Jesus taught:
>   that only what is first broken, like bread,
>   can be shared;
>   that only what is broken
>   is open to your entry;
>   that old wineskins must be ripped open and replaced
>   if the wine of new life is to expand;
>   that only those who show justice and compassion
>   can find new life.[12]

A fourth precondition for doing globalization ethics lies in our struggle to make sense out of the ambiguities and polarities of life; it is the invitation to *name* our own suffering. The moral act of naming one's suffering is a way of knowing and being in the world. I suspect that many marginalized people in the world know that the God of the Bible is one who cares, one who identifies with their sufferings and hurts in the struggle for justice and human dignity. In God's *pathos,* for instance, the ancient Hebrews discovered something amazing about righteousness and compassion. And the scriptures bear witness to God's righteousness and compassion, from generation to generation, especially toward the poor and the marginalized. Like much of the prophetic literature, Psalm 37 contains many statements that *name* the reality:

The wicked draw the sword and bend their bows,
to bring down the poor and needy,
to slay those who walk uprightly;
their sword shall enter their own heart,
and their bows shall be broken.

(vv. 14–15)

Notice how the psalmist continues the act of naming by issuing a strong directive or ethical imperative to the saints of God:

Depart from evil, and do good;
so shall you abide forever
For the Lord loves justice;
[God] will not forsake [God's] saints.

(vv. 27–28)

We may say then that through the radical act of naming the "evil" or the "good," the "wicked" or the "righteous," globalization ethics can evoke greater faithfulness and integrity in people. In naming, we lay bare our souls before the mercy and compassion of God. Finally, whatever the trial or tribulation, whatever the sin or injustice, whatever the failure or the betrayal, biblical faith teaches us simply to name our tragic circumstances. Why? Because any viable framework for doing globalization ethics must necessarily remind us that God always cares about the moral details of our lives. In the global community, God cares about all the pain, suffering, hopes, and triumphs we encounter in the moral struggle to be faithful and free. Concerning the ultimate triumph of moral struggle, that is, the promise of God's sustaining presence with us through all ages under the sun, an African proverb poignantly says: "Only those who have been tried in the fire will not scorch in the sun." Fundamentally, what I suggest is this: The liberating core of faith is *born in the fire!*

9

ETHICAL NORMS AND CONTEXTS

What ought I do as a follower of Christ? To answer this question, one is likely to be challenged by the issue of contextuality. The Christian who struggles with problems of survival in the work-a-day world cannot, in good conscience and fairness, separate the issue of standards from the social context in which actions occur. By definition, "standards" refers to provisional norms by which we judge the behavior and actions of people as moral agents. Put another way, a standard is a norm of judgment to which human moral action is subjected. If we believe that Christ is the norm or model for moral life, then it is reasonable to assume that, in the light of the gospel as good news for the poor, as such a norm he must have something to say about the suffering, oppression, and pain that fill our world.

In *The Gospel and the Poor,* Wolfgang Stegemann reflects on the normative importance of the gospel in relation to the poor.[13] Stegemann begins with a discussion of poverty in the Gospels, underscoring Jesus' enormous significance to the needy and the destitute. He points out that the central drama of the gospel occurs around Jesus Christ as Norm and Sustainer of the poor and the weak, as evidenced in his identifying with their suffering, which brings an expression of hope.[14] The global implication of the gospel is apparent. In Stegemann's words, "The gospel is the basis and expression of the hope, self-consciousness, and solidarity among the poor themselves."[15] In the kind of world in which we live, where critical issues of faith and culture, and wholeness and brokenness force Christians to see afresh the image of the global village, the idea of standards becomes central. They inform our fundamental understanding of biblical faith and the freeing grace of God revealed in Jesus Christ as the one for "the poor" and all peoples in the global community. Stegemann describes this new self-understanding succinctly:

> The relationship of Christians, churches and theologians to global poverty no longer concerns merely Christianly self-evident charitable practice: It is becoming, rather, a question of Christian self-understanding. At issue is not merely a practical consequence of our faith in the saving revelation of God in Jesus Christ; at issue is this faith itself.[16]

For the community of faith, the idea of standards is related to the social issue of contextuality. Therefore, from an ethical perspective, there is a logical and creative tension between normativity and contextuality in globalization ethics. Indeed, both critical moral thought and faith arise from and are shaped by the social context in which we understand God, the church, and the world. Christian ethicist Paul Lehmann has made a powerful case for the importance of contextuality. In *Ethics in a Christian Context,* he argues against a purely philosophical approach of moral reasoning and in favor of the "human indicative" emanating from the *koinonia.*[17] For sojourners, struggling pilgrims, and tired followers of Christ in the world, the *koinonia* is the place where the naked are clothed, the hungry find food, the lame walk, and the poor hear the gospel preached. For the community of faith engaged in the struggles and problems of the modern world, globalization ethics is gospel ethics. To paraphrase Lehmann, globalization ethics begins with the normative question of the gospel, What am I as a believer in Jesus Christ and a member of the global community to do? For people in the church, I suspect that the What am I to do? question often comes as a surprise. Perhaps the surprise stems, in part, from the declarative nature of the gospel and its clear moral mandates.

A list of moral mandates for our own global awareness must include

1. To do justice in the land, especially in behalf of the poor and the suffering ones in our midst; this theology of praxis is required by God (see Amos 5:21–24)
2. To love God and neighbor (Matt. 22:37–40)
3. To proclaim joyfully the good news to those of low degree (Luke 1:52)
4. The Christian community must set the captives free (Luke 4:18–19)
5. To seek first God's kingdom and God's righteousness (Matt. 6:33)
6. To share one's own faith story relative to God's liberating grace revealed in Jesus Christ (Matt. 11:1–6).

Undoubtedly, there are other ways the Christian may respond to the question, What am I to do? To people in search of truth and ethical clarity in the global community, the liberating word of the gospel is fresh and life-giving. Indeed, it is fresher than the morning dewdrops that kiss the grass and bring life.[18] The gospel is good news in a bad world. The gospel is movement; and God's suffering love for the poor and the oppressed are expressions of this movement. As I see it, in the global community the gospel's aim is twofold: to liberate the poor and the oppressed, and to make disciples of all men and women. Hence, our concrete acts of liberation—performed as discerning and faithful disciples—identify globalization ethics as gospel ethics.

It is through the transforming power of the gospel that globalization ethics must ultimately stake its claim. Therefore, the ethical claims upon us are to follow Christ and to be about the task of "making disciples" of all nations, races, and people throughout the *oikoumene,* the whole of the inhabited earth. What I find amazing about the gospel of Jesus Christ is the centrality of the global imperative for all peoples and cultures.[19]

> Go therefore and make disciples of all nations, baptizing them in the name of the Father and of the Son and of the Holy Spirit, teaching them to observe all that I have commanded you; and lo, I am with you always, to the close of the age. (Matt. 28:19–20)

The authority for discipleship and faithfulness on the part of the church today must rest on nothing less than this global imperative.

USE OF THE CASE STUDY METHOD

The case study method helps us practically to explore the issues of identity, faithfulness, and directionality, and the burden of ethics in Christian moral life. A case is an instrument for understanding the identity of the other and a tool for bridging cultural and religious differences. Louis B. Weeks defines a case as "the relationship of receiving God's vision for ourselves and the world, while responding in discipleship and seeking to grow in character. . . . A case is a written account of an actual situation in the lives of people . . . The purpose of the case is to begin with the instance and to move from that specific example to learn of other situations and resources in more general terms."[20]

The case study method does not permit the vastness and cultural complexity of the global community to be obstacles to understanding. Rather, it encourages and allows the morally sensitive Christian to begin with the particular situation. A case is a concrete way of entering into dialogue with the other and of nurturing values and principles of Christian experience in the world. It is an *inductive* method of moral reasoning and reflection upon critical social, cultural, and religious issues in the life of the human family.

While obvious limitations of time, space, data, and perspective play into the way we share particular cases, I suspect that the consensus among people who use cases is that they broaden our understanding of Christian faith and spiritual maturity in the global community. To be fully "Christian" implies struggling, agonizing, discerning, deciding, and growing in the love and grace of God revealed in Jesus Christ. As Louis Weeks observes, "The case study also assumes God's Spirit at work among us and within us, showing us ways to grow in the faith and ways to proclaim the gospel in our lives."[21]

Steps in Case Study Analysis

Case study analysis must be consistent with the understanding and objectives I have identified. There are systematic steps involved in case analysis which may assist the Christian in working through the moral dilemmas of case material in this book. I provide below some guidelines in the form of ethical questions. These questions are meant as a general suggestive guide to indicate the sort of "boundary questions" one may wish to raise in exploring the cases. They are useful as a tool to aid and sharpen meaningful dialogue and discussion and can clarify our perspective about the phenomenon of globalization. They are not, however, intended as an exclusive list of questions.

1. What are the critical facts of the case?

   Know the facts of the case. While in no case are *all* the facts given, the important ones are. Be able to screen the facts and eliminate unimportant information. It may be necessary to make certain assumptions as the case analysis progresses, but these should be realistic assumptions and should be minimized. The facts will reveal the problem at hand as well as possible alternative courses of action.

2. What is the common ground for genuine dialogue?

   Theological reflection. The Christian believer or moral agent comes to each case with a set of convictions, beliefs, values, and experiences that have been shaped by a particular worldview. Knowing one's own angle of vision is, therefore, both necessary and desirable for genuine theological dialogue. For example, what values do people of diverse cultural heritage share about God, family, church, and the global community?

3. What streams of thought or moral fibers flow through the case?

   Analyze the rhythm of the case. Seek to know the social world or environment in which the case exists. Know what affects the social situation and how. Identify and analyze the salient features in the background of the individuals involved. Ask yourself, for example, what issues you find disturbing in the rhythm of the case.

4. What is going on?

   Know the objectives of the individuals involved. While objectives may not be apparent, realistic ones can often be defined. An apparent lack of objectives may indicate a major problem. How would you likely respond to the objectives and problems of the case from your own faith stance and experience?

5. How does the situational problem of the case relate to universal meanings of life?

   Know and define the major problem(s). While the central problem is often readily apparent, that is not always the case. Try to focus upon the central problem, the one which if solved would alleviate many others. Think through the cause-and-effect relationships in the problem. In defining the problem it is important to identify the basic issue involved as made evident by the facts of the case. Ask, for example, What are the starting points for relating the themes of faith and liberation to the major problems of the case? Can doubt or suffering contribute to faith in God?

6. What shall I, as a person of faith and conscience, decide?

   Establish alternative courses of moral action. There are any number of ways to solve a problem. Think of all reasonable courses of action that will solve the problem as defined. This step will require faithfulness to one's own convictions and individual creativity. Your alternatives must necessarily fit within the framework created by the insights of the case. Ask, for example, What are the alternative categories of moral reasoning that may be used in relating the Bible to the critical issues of the case? As a follower of Christ, what am I to do?

7. What form should faith take for the person whose back is against the wall?

   Postcritical reflection. Moral insight and careful discussion about one's faith journey is never complete without the process of postcritical reflection. After the dialogic process of deciding and acting, the moral agent is obligated to assess what has taken place; and in so doing, one can determine the degree to which a fitting response has been achieved. For example, I may decide to change my own views or lifestyle in some way, as a result of self-examination and moral agonizing over questions of oppression and signs of hope in the global community. In short, postcritical reflection evokes further dialogue on alternative actions. Specific ethical questions may include: What constitutes a morally responsible act? How can the act of being morally good increase global awareness? What does the Lord require of me in the light of human suffering and oppression?

SUMMARY

Our discussion on globalization ethics affirms the value of religious and cultural diversity. All people in the global community have dignity and human worth by virtue of our identity as children of God. Therefore, globalization ethics is especially relevant in terms of how middle-class North American Christians can relate to and perceive the issues at stake in Third World and African countries. Such religio-cultural diversity can save the Western church from deadening uniformity and provincialism.

The language of globalization ethics is valuable in that it emphasizes the relationship between *universality* and *contextuality* in the attempt on the part of the morally sensitive person to answer such questions as, What values do people of diverse cultural heritage share? What constitutes a morally responsible act? What am I, as a believer in Jesus Christ and a member of the global community, to do? It is my basic conviction that we are obligated to think theologically about these questions and other concerns if we are to increase ethical sensitivity and our global awareness.

Globalization ethics is a way of thinking and being that seeks to discern the mission of the church in the world as a mission of liberation for the poor and the oppressed. Accordingly, the act of moral discernment for the community of faith involves pondering the critical concerns of social justice, racial and cultural inclusivity, equality, accountability, and a willingness to trust the radical claims of the gospel of Jesus Christ to make all things new.

I have suggested here that the case study method is a useful instrument for understanding the identity of the other as well as a tool for bridging cultural and religious differences among people from divergent social backgrounds. Although a case is a relatively small chunk of reality, discussing and analyzing it can, nevertheless, help us in our struggle with the critical moral issues of our time. I believe that the use of cases in the global community of ethical discourse enables the Christian to grow spiritually through the dialogic process of agonizing, discerning, deciding, and acting in light of the reality of the gospel of Jesus Christ for the good of suffering humanity.

Globalization ethics has the task of speaking to the realities of pain and human suffering in our world. In this sense, globalization ethics, I have argued, is rooted in more than the moral claims of the gospel. Perhaps more important for the church and its mission in the *oikoumene,* globali-

15

zation ethics is *gospel ethics*. The final appeal must rest upon faith in the promises of God's liberating and reconciling acts in Jesus Christ.

> In Christ Jesus, you who once were far off have been brought near in the blood of Christ. For he is our peace, who has made us both one, and has broken down the dividing wall of hostility. (Eph. 2:13–14)

NOTES

1. Yoshiro Ishida, *Report: A Center for Global Mission, Feasibility Study* (Lutheran School of Theology at Chicago, Fall edition, 1988). Ishida seems to possess a deep commitment to the emerging theme of globalization and its impact on indigenous churches and people of color the world over. While crosscultural and mission studies appear to be emphasized at the Center, Ishida and his colleagues also seem to provide ecumenical leadership on the critical question of "globalization" locally in the metropolitan Chicago area. To broaden one's global awareness of the pain and promise of the gospel in the world, see Kosuke Koyama, *Three Mile an Hour God* (Maryknoll, N.Y.: Orbis Books, 1979).

2. Donald W. Shriver, Jr., "The Globalization of Theological Education: Setting the Task," *Theological Education* (Spring 1986): 8–11. Here Shriver issues a basic challenge to theological schools, churches, and morally concerned theologians to take a serious look at the import of Christian faith for the "entirety of humankind." Thus Shriver argues that throughout the *oikoumene*, the critical ethical task involves nothing less than breaking down the "dividing walls of hostility" as the proper expression of our faithfulness to God and the liberating gospel of Jesus Christ.

3. See Ngugi Wa Thiong'o, *Homecoming: Essays on African and Caribbean Literature, Culture and Politics* (Nairobi, Kenya: Heinemann Educational Books, 1972), 3–21.

4. Gayraud S. Wilmore, "Theological Education in a World of Religious and Other Diversities," *Association of Theological Schools Theological Education Supplement* 23 (1987): 142–56.

5. John C. Bennett, *The Radical Imperative: From Theology to Social Ethics* (Philadelphia: Westminster Press, 1975), 35.

6. Ibid., 28.

7. Ibid., 45.

8. Shriver, "Globalization of Theological Education," 8.

9. Charles L. Kammer, *Ethics and Liberation: An Introduction* (Maryknoll, N.Y.: Orbis Books, 1988), 11–12. In this volume, Kammer explores the practical value of Christian ethics for addressing contemporary issues ranging from oppression and economic exploitation to health care and nuclear disarmament. This book is strongly recommended for students and pastors who struggle with the agony of moral decisionmaking in the conflicting faith claims in our global village.

10. Stanley Hauerwas, *A Community of Character* (Notre Dame: Ind.: University of Notre Dame Press, 1981). This book provides the reader with a constructive understanding of Christian ethics rooted in the *narrative* claims of biblical faith in its relation to "character" in the shaping of the moral life in the world. In

terms of global awareness, the core of Hauerwas's thesis regarding the gospel of Jesus Christ and the ethical presence of the church in the world is the claim that we are a "story-formed community." Here he argues that narrative is the central category for doing social ethics in a world where Christians and non-Christians alike are called to resist the evil of injustice and human oppression, as we trust in God's promise of redemption and wholeness. Hence, "character ethics" requires on the part of the church and all people conscience to share their stories of faith and moral struggle (see pp. 9–18).

11. Kammer, *Ethics and Liberation,* 188.

12. Cited in Eden Seminary chapel, "New Wineskins and Dreams" (Eden Theological Seminary, November 1988).

13. See Wolfgang Stegemann, *The Gospel and the Poor* (Philadelphia: Fortress Press, 1984).

14. Ibid., 22.

15. Ibid.

16. Ibid., 64.

17. Paul Lehmann, *Ethics in a Christian Context* (New York: Harper & Row, 1963), 45–49. Lehmann explores the nature and structure of Christian ethics with the idea of *koinonia* as the central interpretive category for moral discourse as faithfulness to the claims of God in the world. Methodologically, his point of departure is with the question: What am I, as a believer in Jesus Christ and as a member of his church, to do? For Lehmann, the idea of *koinonia* provides the believer with a response to the question by suggesting that we do "the will of God" contextually. Hence, the idea of *koinonia* shapes both the perception and one's contextual response to the will of God in the global community in the interest of liberation and "to bring about human maturity" (p. 117).

18. Enoch H. Oglesby, *God's Divine Arithmetic* (Nashville: Townsend Press, 1985), 28ff.

19. See Francis C. Arinze, "Globalization of Theological Education," *Association of Theological Schools Theological Education* 23 (Autumn 1986): 8–27.

20. Louis B. Weeks, *Making Ethical Decisions: A Casebook* (Philadelphia: Westminster Press, 1987), 36–37.

21. Ibid., 37–38.

2

FOLK PROVERBS AND
FAITH FORMATION

So faith comes from what is heard, and what is heard comes by the
preaching of Christ. (Rom. 10:17)

STORYTELLING AND FAITH

Ask any Christian in the African-American community about the
importance of the Bible as a source of *faith* and you will likely be told
that the Bible is the living word of God. The Bible does not present the
Christian with a collection of systematic reflections about the signs and
wonders of life. To the contrary, it presents us with a *way* of life, a way
of hearing and responding, a way of groping and coping, a way of telling
our own story, and a way of suffering and being set free as a people of
God.

The Bible also lays before us the *story* of God's liberating activity
among people of faith. This storytelling draws upon our imaginations and
invites us to "come along" as active participants in the surprising drama
of God's creation. It invites believers into a context in which to hear and
see God in new ways. We see and hear—as we journey through human
life—in ways we have not seen or heard before. The combination of
storytelling and faith enables us to discern the movements of the spirit of
God in human community. We can then affirm in the words of scripture
that "so faith comes from what is heard, and what is heard comes by the
preaching of Christ" (Rom. 10:17).

It is my conviction that individual "faith" and character are shaped, in
part, by the proverbs we hear from elders or others important to us. I

believe that certain proverbs, that is, the sayings and stories we tell to one another in human community, mirror faith formation. The stories we tell, the images we hold, the theological claims we affirm are not morally neutral. They are value-centered responses to the sociocultural context in which we live, move, and have our being.

Storytelling and faith come together precisely at the juncture of struggle and hope, of pain and promise, of vulnerability and discernment of God's liberating grace in the lives of suffering people the world over. Storytelling can be a way of experiencing, struggling, nurturing, and growing in faith. It is a way to say symbolically, We want to share our heart and soul . . .''; ''Join in the circle of God's love and favor . . .''; or ''Brothers and sisters, let's talk about our struggles from the inside out.''

The starting point of storytelling is, therefore, *our own story* of faith. Faith is not a set of intellectual concepts about the being and nature of God vis-à-vis the tragic accidents of human history. Faith is not an abstract theological truth that somehow saves us as a result of contemplative toil, nor is it a majestic prize that we win at the end of life because we have been ''good'' people who have followed a prescribed set of moral rules in society. Faith is not even conformity of the mind to an object or legitimate authority in the contemporary world. Rather, faith comes by hearing the stories of the people of God, by being open to God's redemptive story in Jesus Christ, and by making a radical commitment to follow Jesus Christ, the one whose divine story sets us free. Storytelling indicates an openness of the self to the lessons of the heart and to the rhythm of the Spirit inside of us.

Faith is an invitation to the process of transformation, as Christians seek to discern God's liberating love and truth in their own lives in the service of humankind. Storytelling moves on two levels in faith formation. At the narrative level is the story of a people's relationship to God and the nurturing of that relationship through the social traditions of the past. The second level is the *interpersonal* level, the way in which God makes known God's own liberating will in the actual experiences, beliefs, promises, failures, and hopes of suffering people as they live their own stories in human community the world over.

STORYTELLING AND LIBERATION

Storytelling puts faith in tension with earthly powers. Through reading and sharing faith in human community, we know that the revelation of God's liberating story takes place within the context of real people, with real problems, in real communities. We know that life is heavily burdened with evil, injustice, and oppression. At a time, for example, when the economic gap between black and white, male and female, skilled and unskilled, rich countries and poor countries appears to be widening in the world community, no simple moralism about the character of faith will do. No universal theory of Christian love can quiet or drown out the sounds of struggle by oppressed people for liberation, nor soften the pain of injustice, violence, neglect, and the constant assault on the human spirit. Today, the cry of faith—whether in Africa, Asia, Latin America, North America—is the cry of those who have been abandoned: the poor, the homeless, the hungry, the powerless, and the faceless masses who are often stigmatized by their competitive society and called "losers"; they have nowhere to turn and no one to turn to except God. Today, the cry of faith is the cry from the bottom, from the underside of history. Some believe that such a cry of faith has meaning only to those who will bother to listen, to listen, that is, to the voice of God in the rhythm of the life stories of those who suffer, bleed, and die for their dignity. The cry of faith is the cry for liberation and human wholeness. It is an understanding of the living word of God as the raison d'être that summons us to be engaged in struggle against the "principalities and powers" and for the sake of a world born in love and justice.

Storytelling and liberation theology enable the Christian community to understand faith in the light of God's solidarity with the poor and the oppressed. Liberation theology, for instance, speaks to the conditions of oppression in our world. We believe that God sides with the poor and oppressed not because they are more moral or virtuous than others—for surely scripture reminds us that all have sinned—but rather because of God's own compassion and steadfast love for the weak and vulnerable. It has been said that liberation is the root of *who God is* in Jesus Christ. For the poor and oppressed, Jesus is Liberator. As Christians, we are challenged to be in ministries of compassion and liberation because of what and who God is, and because of what God has done for us in the story of Jesus Christ. In this sense, to be a Christian means to stand with those who have "no standing" and to tell our own penultimate stories of faith in a world where women and men are crucified daily on the crosses of poverty, despair, greed, and human exploitation.

FOLK PROVERBS AND FAITH IN AFRICAN AND AFRICAN-AMERICAN COMMUNITIES

As I have noted, faith is the occasion to hear and share in each other's stories and in the power of God's liberating word in our daily lives. Now we simply ask, How goes the drama of faith in the African and African-American communities? I would argue that the formation of faith in these communities is not unrelated to the folk culture, social values and beliefs, wisdom sayings, and proverbs that traditionally give shape to one's identity as a Christian believer. For example, most African societies have historically had rich traditions of folk sayings and proverbs, which were a means of providing social control and moral guidance in a village community. They were used to demonstrate and cultivate certain virtues that implied the formation of good character before God and community. Indeed, one's knowledge of the nature of God and of faith itself is often expressed in *proverbs*. In his book *African Religions and Philosophy*, John S. Mbiti discusses the importance of proverbs in shaping religious and social life:

> African knowledge of God is expressed in proverbs, short statements, songs, prayers, names, stories and religious ceremonies. All of these are easy to remember and pass on to other people, since there are no sacred writings in traditional societies.[1]

In every culture, proverbs image reality in some way. By indirectly symbolizing the boundary of traditional morality held by individual people in a given society, they tell us something about ourselves, the nature of God and community, and the structure of faith and character. I suspect that proverbs may influence the way we teach and raise our children in the home, the way we choose to relate to each other in the neighborhood, and, inevitably, the way we hear and speak the gospel of Jesus Christ in the global community.

The "proverb" is one of the most ancient forms of folklore.[2] Its full significance in the history and context of African-American experience is difficult to discern. J. Mason Brewer has observed that proverbs have both religious and social insights into the nature of the human condition and probably can be best interpreted metaphorically.[3] Proverbs are relevant in three ways to our understanding of the themes of faith and liberation in the lives of individuals and in the case studies.

1. Folk proverbs are rooted in the social, cultural, and religious context of a people. For Africans and African-American, they tend to function as guideposts to the expression of faith in God and the celebration of human life, despite the misfortunes, injustices, and contradictions of the present social situation.

2. Folk proverbs often possess the power to shape identity and faith by mirroring a reality that is "not yet" but "might be." In other words,

the simple sayings of certain proverbs may point us toward the truth of how to better live our daily lives in faithfulness to God and love of neighbor.

3. Folk proverbs are tensive and elastic. By this I mean that they may provide us with prophetic imagination and courage in responding to the incongruities and problems, the trials and tribulations that come to us in life. In times of crisis, for example, proverbs may help to give hope to the hopeless and create feelings of solidarity among the suffering.

Many of the case studies in this book reflect an appreciation for the functional value of the proverb in understanding the dynamics of faith and human pilgrimage. While many social historians and religion scholars hold the view that a majority of African proverbs were apparently lost in America because of the ordeal of slavery, some *did* survive. Their subtle influence can be seen throughout the rich African-American tradition of folk tales, work songs, and spirituals.

SHARED TRADITIONS

Similarities exist between the struggles of black people in Africa and the United States for self-determination, dignity, equality, and a sense of faithfulness to a freeing and unfailing God. Parallels between such experiences can often be easily drawn. Identifying parallels between proverbs from different continents is more difficult.

In line with my earlier discussion of storytelling, proverbs, and faith formation, I have identified seven African proverbs and seven African-American proverbs relevant to the themes of faith and liberation. The proverbs, which follow, alternate, one from the African continent, the next from the North American.

I do not make comparisons between the groups. Rather, by alternating or pairing them, I suggest that they contain elements of continuity, that there are links and similarities between them. Our mutual challenge is to make sense of each of these idiomatic expressions in ways that work for the modern world. I challenge you to reflect on the links between the proverbs, on the similarities among our experiences.

1. I am because we are, and since we are, therefore, I am.[4]

This proverb is both common and popular in African society. It is a way for people to understand African history, culture, religion, ethics, art, esthetics, economics, and the politics of human relationships. On an ethical level, it presupposes that personhood and character are formed *only* in community, as individuals interact with one another. For example, a person's own faith or worldview is not good or bad, right or wrong in any abstract sense; it is, instead, valuable only in relation to standards of conduct prescribed by community. This proverb would suggest that for the African Christian "love" is not a virtue until people actually demonstrate that love through the bonds of kinship and hospitality. Individual faith and identity spring from corporate awareness, as each person is accountable to God and community for his or her own acts, gifts, talents, properties, and blessings.

The importance of "we-consciousness" was brought home to me by an incident involving a village fisherman in Mombasa, Kenya. My friend Tossou had gone out rather early in the morning to fish in a nearby forest lake. I noticed that he left with one bucket and a pole, but later in the afternoon he returned with two buckets and a pole. Curious, I inquired about the matter and he explained simply, "When one man goes fishing in our village, two families eat."

What is interesting to observe in this story is that Tossou's traditional values and religion insisted that acts of love and hospitality best reflect what faith in God really means. As John Mbiti rightly points out, "The essence of African morality is that it is more 'seceder' than 'spiritual'; it is a morality of 'conduct' rather than a morality of 'being.' "[5] Hence, this folk proverb underscores the kinship nature of identity and faith in the struggle for liberation and wholeness as a people of God.

2. We ain't what we oughtta be;
   we ain't what we wanna be;
   we ain't what we gonna be;
   but thank God,
   we ain't what we was.[6]

This African-American proverb expresses the reality, yearning, and hope of a people still in formation. It gives imaginative expression to the scandalous faith of the "old ones" gone before who had given up neither on themselves nor on God's future of freedom with them. Obviously, such a proverb speaks for itself. As a people of faith, perhaps we always move forward by looking where we have come from. Perhaps this folk proverb will help us continue to do just that. Given the exigency of our present reality, such a proverb may remind us, in the words of a popular gospel song, to better affirm each other by saying, "Please be patient with me; God is not through with me yet!"

African-American Christians are painfully aware of negative forces or obstacles that work against their becoming what they "ought to be." These obstacles include the cultural elements of racism, sexism, and the glorification of a "Rambo mentality" but also the demoralizing personal self-hate and low self-esteem that depress the human spirit. But, despite the complexity of contemporary social and moral issues, the overwhelming message of this proverb pertains: God is still at work today in the minds and souls of blacks and of all people of good will, renewing and mending broken lives and forever calling us to faithfulness and accountability. In the storytelling and oral tradition of the elders, we can proverbially affirm—with shouts of divine praise—that "we ain't what we was." For brothers and sisters to say just that is a sign of hope.

In this African-American proverb, popularized in the civil rights movement by Martin Luther King, Jr., over two decades ago, we see a dynamic people on the march, striving to become all they can be. I suspect that the powerful image of this proverb is a testimony not only to the radiance of the human spirit under the yoke of a legacy of slavery, but a way of understanding events through the eyes of faith in a God who cares.

3. No one shows a child the Supreme Being.

In the light of the divine-human encounter, the wisdom of this African saying is very special to the Christian community. It is a way of saying that no human being is entirely devoid of a God-consciousness, a sense of Presence inside of oneself that gives life meaning and purpose. Here the image is of the tender innocence and laughter of a child, a child who is awake to the presence of God while playing, dreaming, and interacting with others in the context of home and village life. The folk proverb suggests that even a child knows and is known by the Supreme Being. Faith is nurtured in this knowledge of Presence and the openness engendered by the affirmations of children in the world. Here I agree with Mbiti's assertion that children know God exists almost by their own nature and instinct.[7]

If this is the case, the question before us can be morally disturbing: How well do parents and teachers listen to the voices of children? Perhaps the wider theological implication of this proverb for our own faith journey is the question of how well we provide a ministry of listening for those in need in our society. Furthermore, the proverb may trigger in us the invitation to grapple more seriously with the significant role children played in the way Jesus of Nazareth symbolized the coming of the kingdom. Said Jesus to his disciples, "Truly, I say to you, unless you turn and become like children, you will never enter the kingdom of heaven. Whoever humbles [themselves] like this child, [s]he is the greatest in the kingdom of heaven" (Matt. 18:3–4).

In terms of proverbial wisdom and faith, it was to the children, the innocent ones, the poor, the simple and unburdened souls without station or rank that the spirit of God's kingdom was revealed. This folk proverb shows that the disinherited had, in fact, inherited the supreme gift: the image of the kingdom joyfully mirrored on the faces of children. So it is little wonder that the African proverb heralds, "No one shows a child the Supreme Being!" Thus God must have had something very profound in mind to teach us about the formation of faith as expressed through the lives of children. I was struck by a moving line in the gospel song near the end of the movie, *The Color Purple*, which depicted for me the paradox and promise of faith in black life. To paraphrase the song, it went, "Listen, please listen, God may be trying to tell you something." In short, God's proverbial wisdom may be tested within us by how well we pay attention to our children and their carefree expressive faith. For they may be trying to tell us something.

4. De Lord, my child, sees from behind the shell.

This African-American proverb was brought to my attention by the Reverend Rufus Taylor, an old-time Baptist preacher who lives in Lynn, Massachusetts. We spoke in the early 1970s, during my work as a student minister of a small New England congregation in the black community. The occasion for our conversation was a week of autumn revival and evangelism sponsored by our church. We felt that it was important then, as it is now, to keep alive the spirit of hope and active involvement in the community about issues of social justice and human dignity. Looking back, I must confess that though our zeal and passion often lacked some realism, they were never without meaningful symbols and proverbial expression.

Taylor was a man of humble beginnings who came North from the Mississippi Delta after World War II. As with many of his generation, he came in search of a better way of life for himself and his growing family. He worked at the General Electric Company, and while he never pastored a church on his own, he did evangelistic work in the Lynn community. As a devoted Christian, Mr. Taylor never forgot his "down home" experiences, folk beliefs, and ethical teachings about right and wrong. According to Taylor, this proverb, "De Lord, my child, sees from behind the shell," meant that God's all-seeing eyes could penetrate the "outward appearances and fancy clothes that important-acting folks ofttimes wear to church to establish their own goodness."

For this old-time preacher, the proverb was a warning against the social forms of idolatry in the community of the faithful; a warning to church folks not to be hypocrites and pretenders—for God can see from "behind the shell." God can *unmask* the mask we all wear. In terms of one's life pilgrimage and the nurture of faith, it is a proverbial warning against all forms of "showboat" religion that may induce a noisy shout on Sunday morning but are powerless to speak to the problems of the human condition on Monday morning. Thus it seems to me that Taylor's pithy words call each one to accountability for the inner life and integrity of the self before God.

5. Every bird flies with its own wings.

Most of the people I talked with in the African church community of Kenya did not see this folk proverb as a mandate to "do your own thing." Rather, to them it was a way for the believer to assert from the heart that the practice of faith and the struggle for liberation must be part of each person's work done for the sake of the whole community. For example, when one man or woman is busy at work on the *shamba* (land), tilling the soil and sowing seeds of corn in order to reap a good harvest, the neighbors in the village do not just sit by in idleness. Rather, they all join in to produce a bigger harvest for the entire village.

The folk wisdom of village life requires a contribution from each person. Each is *expected* to "flap his [her] own wings" for the good of the whole. This Swahili saying may not differ that much from the Marxist axiom, "From each according to ability, to each according to need." We all know that ability and need vary from one person to the next. The upshot of this African saying, however, is the recognition that a given gem of proverbial wisdom—in relation to such an axiomatic Marxist concept—cannot do justice to the critical concerns of all people. What is at stake in this African saying is the spirit of self-initiative, or so it seems to me. We may safely assume that in matters of faith and struggle, each person in traditional African society has some responsibility for his or her own conduct, behavior, and deeds. For the young, certain rites of initiation and passage underscored the importance of this folk proverb among village people.

6. Every tub must sit on its own bottom.

The fundamental religious and moral perspectives of Africa continue to impact the lives of African-Americans through the tradition of proverbs and oral sayings. We cannot say with historical accuracy that in its present form this particular proverb is a unique idiomatic saying from the African heritage. In the ongoing debate among historians, sociologists, and religion scholars about remnants of African culture in the African diaspora, many hold that sayings of this type were already a part of their tradition when slaves finally reached America. This line of sociohistorical reasoning argues that the demands of survival and adaptation produced such proverbs or wisdom sayings. Others maintain that similar proverbial sayings were actually brought to the new world by slaves themselves and then were modified to meet the moral challenges of chattel slavery.

Regardless of the proverb's historical origins, it seems clear that African-Americans have always had a strong sense of independence, imagination, and industry in providing for the needs of the self, the family, and the community. While blacks in American society have worked in concert to achieve the broader goal of freedom, the obligation for individual responsibility has been no less crucial. The language of this proverb accents the importance of individual responsibility for the sake of the self and community.

This saying implies that for African-American Christians faith in God must move beyond pious feelings to a higher level of obedience to Christ and the moral command that "every person must bear their own burden" (Gal. 6:5). According to proverbial wisdom and faith, God's promises do not exclude us from individual responsibility. A line from a gospel song expresses nicely this proverbial sentiment: "Must Jesus bear the cross alone and all the world go free? No, there is a cross for everyone, and there is a cross for me." In short, African-American Christianity affirms the inseparability of freedom and responsibility in the daily lives of black people.

7. The eyes of a frog never stopped the cow from drinking water.

This proverb was shared with me by Peter P. K. Njoroge, a Kikuyu elder who lives in the central province of Kenya. For a number of years Mr. Njoroge has worked with the poorest rural Kenyans, seeking to preserve the religious and cultural heritage of village people. He has an acute interest in the religio-cultural legacy of the elders, and the way in which certain traditions are passed on to the younger generation.

The proverb is set against the backdrop of village life. It appears that the saying grew out of a period of British colonial rule when people experienced great suffering and exploitation. (At least this was the report given to me by a local villager.) Such a proverb would be spoken in rural and urban settings alike, among the poor as well as the better educated Kenyans who valued their heritage and moral stuggle. While its meaning depends on the social context in which it is used, Njoroge interpreted the proverb in the following manner: "The white settlers often came with the roaming eyes of the frog. . . . They took our land but later had to give it up because the 'cow' proved to be wiser than the frog. Now eventually all the frog could do was to watch the cow drink freely, once again, from his own pond."

Another elder said, concerning this proverb, "One should pay no attention to the envious eyes of the watchman, just be your own doer." The African Christian, clearly, is admonished here to give no place to idle or evil work, but keep your eyes fixed on the good works in God's kingdom.

8. 'People raving about hard times—
   tell me what it's all about?
   Hard times don't worry me,
   I was broke when they started out.[8]

An example of poetic folklore, this African-American folk proverb is actually taken from a traditional blues verse. Its beauty and poetic content speak for themselves.[9] The proverb expresses the impulse in the human spirit to dismantle anxiety and take the cutting edge off sorrow and disappointment. African-Americans have recognized and celebrated this impulse as they have sought to survive and find meaning in a world not fully their own. At a spiritual level, this saying is a poetic expression of the strength of faith in black life. It is a testimony to the reality that black folks have always been acquainted with the crucible of hard times, borne their sorrows in the heat of the day, shouted their stories of protest and hope, and prayed to their God for endurance and deliverance.

I suspect that this proverb reveals a particular characteristic of African-American experience and religious belief. It seems to whisper that the burden of hard times will inevitably knock on every person's door. Every human being must answer the knock. The proverbial scenario suggests that there is no escape; so "tell me what it's all about?" For the faithful believer in the God who delivers, this does not mean either a fatalistic surrender to the groaning of human suffering or a sort of acquiescence to the fiery furnace of hard times. Rather it expresses assurance that God will deliver. Therefore, "hard times don't worry me." The plight of blacks in America has been difficult and the loads on their backs heavy. But for children of faith and struggle, the proverbial question or instinctive musing cannot be ignored: Why sink down into the mire of self-pity? "After all I was broke when hard times started out . . . and man, the only way to go is up, when you're already on the bottom!"

Of course, for the faithful the true wisdom of this saying is not to give in to self-pity. As deliverance came to the motherless and fatherless in ancient days, so it will come to us in God's own good time, if we remain faithful despite the bitter sorrow often experienced by blacks in America.

Such a proverbial expression of hope is also found in the psalmist's declaration:

I wait for the Lord, my soul waits,
   and in [the Lord's] word I hope;
my soul waits for the Lord
   more than watchmen for the morning.
                              (Psalm 130:5–6)

9. If you chase me out with a stick, I'll come back with a bigger stick, but if you chase me out with the truth, I will not come back.

In my research and conversations with African people, especially in Kenya, I was struck by the frequent use of this proverb or saying. It incorporates a dynamic theme of African religion and culture. It embodies a burning faith in God and in the hope of liberation from all forms of human oppression.

I found this folk proverb in common use by elders of the Kikuyu, particularly in rural village settings of the central province of Kenya. As one elder proudly explained to me, "Our tough fight for independence in our country could not go sour, because we had 'truth' and righteousness on our side. And the 'sticks' of the adversary were not big enough to defeat our cause. When many of our warriors were without guns, the elders used their walking canes as symbols of rebellion and hope. We chased them out with the stick of 'truth' in our cause."

The theological wisdom of this proverb is simply that the bonds of truth are ultimately stronger than the brutal "sticks" of oppression and exploitation. The first part of the saying is motivated by a lust for power; the latter part of the saying is inspired by an insatiable thirst for truth rooted in God and the life struggles of individual Christians. The meaning of the proverb was expressed to me by other elders of the community as being, "He who is driven away by a club returns, but he who is driven away by justice does not return."[10]

This proverb may also express the Africans' faith in a God who enters the concrete affairs and struggles of the oppressed for the sake of justice and truth. The proverb images an alternative reality that is rooted not in power or privilege but in love and truth, as Africans affirm new dimensions of their own heritage as a people of God. The tough but universal insight of the proverb cannot be expressed better than in Jesus' remark to his disciples:

And you will know the truth, and the truth will make you free. (John 8:32)

10. Don't crow tel yuh git out o'de woods; dey mought be uh beah behin' de las' tree.

This African-American saying is a piece of folklore collected by black folklorist J. Mason Brewer and reported in an article entitled, "Old-Time Negro Proverbs."[11] The folk language of the proverb seems to date back to the period of slavery. It is interesting to note that the social, political, and religious overtones of the proverb referred in large measure to the theme of freedom. Of course, to say that "freedom" was the only point of the proverbial musings among slaves of this period would be to miss the point. Certainly, the growth and development of proverbs reflect and speak to the human condition at all levels. For example, we noted earlier proverbs that speak to the art of work and survival, and character and the formation of faith in community life.

However, in the oral tradition and speech patterns of former slaves, the theme of freedom as it is disclosed by certain proverbs had a distinctive character. An example is this proverb, "Don' crow tel yuh git out o'de woods." This pithy saying was about the plight of slaves who tried to escape to freedom. Brewer explained the meaning of this proverb: "Don't be careless about talking to people you see, until you get to the Underground Railway; you might get caught and returned to your owner."[12] The injunction here to slaves who risked all for the sake of freedom was clear: keep your eyes open, your mouth shut, and your feet steady on the course of freedom's path. Among slaves the proverb was a sort of code to warn against the danger of "loose lips" or tattling tongues, which are downfalls for those who secretly work for freedom.

This proverb, then, is representative of that group of proverbs that clothed the message of freedom in phrases and songs that slave masters often dismissed as purely benign social entertainment or religious otherworldliness. Undoubtedly, this was part of the genius of the folklore and religion of people of African descent.

11. The enemy prepares a grave, but God prepares you a way of escape.[13]

Storytelling and folklore are forms of communication and relatedness that all cultures share. And all social groups have pivotal corporate moments or "exodus events" that mark the rhythm of their own history from slavery to freedom, from fragmentation to wholeness, from promise to fulfillment. This is such a universal proverb. It mirrors the experiences and struggles of many individuals and social groups in our troubled world, and it seems to put into historical perspective our sense of memory and the hand of God as a guiding force of deliverance. Because God is perceived as a Deliverer and Giver of life in African culture, we are therefore accountable to God. The biblical story of God's deliverance of Israel expresses the same proverbial wisdom in its description of how Yahweh snatched the people from affliction and bondage (Deut. 26:5–9).

We also see in this proverb a sign of the kingdom, in which the enemy is defeated and the cries of the poor are vindicated by a compassionate God. As for traditional African culture, this is always a high moment of celebration in village life. To speak of a compassionate God in the context of village life means that the God of biblical faith identifies with the hurts and hopes of people who suffer oppression and injustice. A compassionate God, I believe, is one who cares about us all. Perhaps the enduring wisdom inherent in this particular proverb is the feeling of gratitude and praise to a God who is faithful and will deliver. The words of the psalmist emphatically declare:

Blessed be the Lord,
    who has not given us
    as prey to their teeth!
We have escaped as a bird
    from the snare of the fowlers;
the snare is broken,
    and we have escaped!
            (Psalm 124:6–7)

33

12. Shout the glad tidings o'er Egypt's dark sea.
     Jehovah has triumphed, his people are free!

The themes of faith, struggle, and deliverance permeate the value system of African-American Christians. For example, in the corpus of slave songs, prayers, sermons, rituals, and sayings, the idea of the promise of freedom—to be enjoyed by the community of the oppressed—abounded. As had their African ancestors, black slaves understood their struggle in the context of divine authority and with the deep feeling that God had ordained no race of people to acquiesce to the brutality of chattel slavery and oppression. Thus, real faithfulness meant rebellion against any oppressive system, because oppression itself is anti-God, since God's own nature is love. The proverbial insight of this saying comes from a verse in the Freedmen's Hymn, and its meaning is the same, in the sense that there is a pattern of continuity with African folk religion and culture. As we look back at their lives under the yoke of slavery, we can see that slaves were courageously bold, as expressed in this classic affirmation:

Oh Freedom! Oh Freedom!
Oh Freedom, I love thee!
And before I'll be a slave,
I'll be buried in my grave,
And go home to my Lord and be free.[14]

13. May God walk you well.

This old Maasai proverb in the form of a prayer evokes the blessed hand of God as a sustaining presence on the dangerous pathways of life. In the Maasai land of Kenya, many of the rural village people raise cattle. To them, a fine herd is not only valuable as a source of food for village households but is also a symbol of wealth and blessing from God. A village person on a journey may mark the path taken by engaging in certain rituals, not the least of which is praying to God for safe travel. But sacrifices and offerings are made, as well, to ensure that things will go well on the journey; animals, elaborate ornaments and objects, even fruits and vegetables can be offered in a sacrificial way to ensure divine favor. Prayers and proverbs, rooted in the wisdom of the people, are daily offered to God to ward off evil, drought, serious sickness, or misfortune along the pathway of one's earthly pilgrimage. An individual warrior may evoke the name of God for well-being on the journey.

So, for the African there are no sacrifices without prayers.[15] Thus we may conclude from this proverb, "May God walk you well," that good fortune for the sojourner is incomplete without prayerfully evoking the name of God.

14. If I laugh loud enough,
    maybe no one will hear me cry.

There is a profound, disarming, and shattering truth in this saying familiar to many people of African descent. It points to a condition in which many who are deeply burdened by the shackles of poverty, oppression, and human misery have to mask their feelings of rage in order not to drown in their own tears. Despite their travail, African-Americans believed that one day "King Jesus will wipe all tears from our eyes!" In other words, the cries and tears that fall are muffled utterances known only to King Jesus, the compassionate one who walked this road before, who knows that we laugh as we cry and cry as we laugh. It is King Jesus who understands the pain and anguish of the disinherited who live each day with their backs against the wall. The irony of the religion of "King Jesus" is that it speaks a word of hope and promise into the lives of the disinherited, which gives them power to overcome the world.[16] This African-American proverb is strikingly expressive of the contemporary life of black people in the wider culture.

SUMMARY

In the African-American heritage, proverbs say something in a profoundly human way about a people fully acquainted with grief and sorrow, but not subdued by them. They do this in four ways. First, the character of our social life in the black religious community has been marked by the use of proverbs. Here it is marked not so much by a singular vision of reality as by the twin shadows of love and hate, acceptance and rejection, freedom and oppression, despair and hope, promise and the longing for fulfillment. If there is a fragile thread that holds together the core of black life, it is this spiritual and moral longing to see more clearly between the shadows, and to better understand not the whys of suffering, but our own weak, fragile responses to others who also cry. In a theological sense, it seems to me that these proverbs beg the question, Can we any longer hear or see beneath the laughter? Perhaps the answer we give to this question, whether tutored or untutored, may determine the issues at stake in the formation of faith, in the struggle for liberation and human wholeness, and in the search for common ground among all people of the global community.

Second, I believe that the proverb itself is a universal positive clue, too long ignored, in our theological understanding of the dimensions and creative tensions of faith and life. Proverbs are meaningful for the Christian community, in that they increase our global awareness as we struggle with critical life and death issues of faith. Global awareness must begin with reverence for human life as a gift of God. Thus, folk proverbs not only can inform our feelings and perceptions about God but also shape our fundamental life orientation as persons. And, as I have stated, my basic conviction in this discussion has been that the formation of faith and moral character in the life of the individual is positively shaped by certain proverbs, which are heard and retold within the community.

Third, storytelling and faith are interwoven; they are two sides of the same coin. They provide African-American Christians with a moral link to their own African heritage and history.

Finally, it is important to recognize that if Christians learn to listen as a community, in new ways, we can worship, serve, and live in new ways. If we could but listen to the deep sayings of the heart, we would undoubtedly experience renewal and openness as we continue to tell our own stories of faith and struggle about a God of compassion and surprise.

NOTES

1. John S. Mbiti, *African Religions and Philosophy.* (New York: Praeger, 1969), 29. As a scholar in the history of African culture and religion, Mbiti is well known and respected on the academic international scene. His formal writings span over two decades. For further study on the value and import of traditional proverbs, see Charlotte Leslau and Wolf Leslau, *African Proverbs* (White Plains, N.Y.: Peter Pauper Press, 1985). In the African religio-cultural context, the authors make the claim that "proverbs are the daughters of experience" (p. 6).

2. Alan Dundes, ed., *Mother Wit from the Laughing Barrel,* (Englewood Cliffs, N.J.: Prentice-Hall, 1973), 246. For a comparative analysis of the social roots of proverbs in the black community and American society, see Janet C. Bell's, *Famous Black Quotations* (Chicago: Sabayt Publications, 1986) Concerning the impetus for her own work, Bell writes: "This collection of quotations was begun after many unsuccessful attempts to locate specific quotations by African-Americans. . . . Since standard reference works either did not include any quotation by people of African descent, or included only a small fraction . . . I saved what I had found for future use" (p. x).

3. See J. Mason Brewer's essay, "Old Time Negro Proverbs," in Dundes, ed., *Mother Wit from the Laughing Barrel,* 246.

4. Mbiti, *African Religions and Philosophy,* 214.

5. Ibid.

6. Roger D. Abrahams, *Positively Black* (Englewood Cliffs, N.J.: Prentice-Hall, 1970), xi. See also Charles W. Chestnut, *The Marrow of Tradition* (Ann Arbor:

University of Michigan Press, 1969); and Sterling D. Plumpp, *Black Rituals* (Chicago: Third World Press, 1972).

7. Mbiti, *African Religions and Philosophy*, 29.

8. Roger D. Abrahams, *Positively Black* (Englewood Cliffs, N.J.: Prentice-Hall, 1970), 84.

9. Ibid., 84–85.

10. Hannah Wangeri Kinoti, "Aspects of Gikuyu Traditional Morality," (Ph.D. diss., University of Nairobi, 1983), 239.

11. Abrahams, *Positively Black*, 246.

12. Ibid., 248.

13. Mbiti, *African Religions and Philosophy*, 67.

14. James H. Cone, *The Spirituals and the Blues* (New York: Seabury, 1972), 30.

15. Mbiti, *African Religions and Philosophy*, 61.

16. Howard Thurman, *Jesus and the Disinherited* (Richmond, Ind.: Friends United Press, 1976). A prolific writer and religion scholar, Thurman posed the key ethical question for the contemporary church in the world, namely, What is the word of the religion of Jesus to those who stand with their backs against the wall? For Thurman, the answer, in part, can be found in our faithfulness to live by the Spirit of God amidst the contradictions, injustices, and chaos of the present world order (pp. 108–9).

PART 2

CASE STUDIES IN FAITH AND LIBERATION

The first right of a people
who want to be free
is the right to define their own reality.
—*Bill Strickland, poet*

For freedom Christ has set us free;
Stand fast therefore, and do not
submit again to the yoke of slavery.
—*Galatians 5:1*

CASE
1

HOMECOMING: REALITY OR HOPE?

The matters under consideration in this case arise from the struggles and experiences of a young refugee family from Uganda. Charles Byaruhanga is thirty-seven, and his wife, Mary, is thirty-two. Despite the constant stress, fear, and loneliness they feel from living in exile, Charles and Mary are happily married and are the proud parents of five lovely children: Juliet, 13, Julius, 12, Jane, 11, Sarah, 9, and Solomon, 7. In their struggle, they indicated emphatically, the reality of faith and love are the bonds that have held their marriage together for their nine years of dislocation and homelessness.

Charles and Mary grew up in the Ankole District of the western province of Uganda, with cultural and religious roots in the Batoro tribe. They have known each other since early childhood. They described their formative years as "happy, ordinary, and uneventful," and, in a manner of speaking, were normal, healthy African children in this district of approximately 2 million people. This is not to suggest that the average African child in the district of Charles's childhood can be described as "healthy" given the persistent realities of poverty and economic deprivation in this region of Uganda. Charles and Mary, however, had the blessings of good health in early childhood.

The dominant traditional language of the village people in their region was Kinyakole. Many of the village people were cattle raisers, goat and sheep herders, agriculturalists, and craftspeople who ran small rural industries in the Ankole District. The major seasonal crops were coffee and tea. The average monthly income of rural workers and laborers was approximately 1,000 shillings, which provided only the bare minimum for survival: food, clothing, and shelter.

Charles had finished a standard course of public education roughly equivalent to a high school diploma in the United States. Mary's educational level was roughly equivalent to ninth grade in the United States. Protestants, Charles and Mary are Anglican in background, although in the Ankole District there are large numbers of Roman Catholics and Muslims.

Now as we sat and spoke in the modest comfort of their quarters, I eventually asked them, "What events led to your exile from Uganda?" Charles replied, "It all started back in 1981 when the government troops launched an orgy of killing, rape, looting, and rampaging the personal property of village folks who live in our district. It was a horrible thing to go through—with all of the confusion and random shooting by the troops."

Continuing, I asked Charles, "But what happened to you and your family?" He explained, "Well, you must understand that we had a nice brick home in the community where we lived. I had a good job and could afford some things that other people in the village could not afford. I had a job working in customs for the Ugandan government; I also had my own business as a clearing and forwarding manager of goods and merchandise. I earned about 10,000 shillings per month, which was a good income for me and my family . . . I ran my own business without government interference for about seven years. But then, the bottom fell out of the economy, and political instability set in. . . .

"I know you asked us what actually happened. Well, it was a gradual thing. The troops and robbers first came and took our two cars . . . I figured that would be all . . . but then they came back and took our radio, TV, and all of the furniture from our house. . . . Naturally, my wife and children were all frightened by now."

While Charles poured out his heart to me, Mary sat in solitude with tears in her eyes, gazing out of the window, as if she were reliving the experience as her husband spoke.

In a calm yet emotional manner, Charles continued. "We thought that it was all over—I mean the looting, the shooting, and the killing. But the government troops and robbers came a third time around to our house . . . And this time they came for us! There was so much confusion and panic all over our town—people screaming and crying, running everywhere, trying to get away from the soldiers and looters . . . All that I remember is the sound of gunfire everywhere as they raided our house . . . I managed to escape, but my wife and children were still trapped inside."

After the darkness and terror of that night in August 1981, Charles was forced to flee Uganda and go into exile in order to save his life. He fled into the country of Burundi and found shelter in a refugee camp. For nearly two years he did not know the fate of his family left behind in Uganda—whether they were living or dead. During this time, the main channels of public communication were broken, and the mood in Uganda was one of fear and uncertainty as thousands of panic-stricken refugees flooded the borders of Uganda in a desperate move to escape the dreadful bloodletting and destruction. As a refugee in Burundi in this dark moment of the soul, Charles recalled lamenting, "All I can do is pray and hope against the odds that my family is alive." In exile, his moral fiber was now being tested. He described those years as a "test of faith" between "little David" and "big Goliath," the storm of battle! For Charles, his refugee ordeal in Burundi was nothing less than the inner struggle of the soul—with a constant shadow of doubt, yet a flicker of hope that would not die.

Meanwhile, in Uganda, Mary had barely escaped death on the night of the raid. To escape the violence of the government troops and warring factions, Mary headed for the borders of Kenya. The urgency of the situation forced her to leave behind her children, and she did not know their fate or their father's. Indeed, Mary revealed that she took literally nothing with her other than the clothes on her back as she crossed the border from Uganda to Kenya. She eventually found temporary shelter in a refugee camp in the city of Nairobi. By now, more than a year and a half had passed, during which Charles and Mary had not seen or heard from each other. One ray of hope did come amidst the despair, and that was Mary's discovery that her children, miraculously, had been found alive and well by relatives and that they were being cared for by their grandmother. On the other hand, Mary sorrowfully confided to a cousin in Nairobi, "I'm afraid that Charles is already dead."

Meanwhile, the warring parties in Uganda were still fighting. The violence and slaughter of innocent people and beloved neighbors continued to escalate. According to Charles, the Ugandan leaders' lust for power has plummeted the nation into political and economic turmoil, thereby increasing and prolonging suffering. Such a state of political affairs is sadly captured in the Swahili proverb, "Where elephants fight, the reeds get hurt!" (Wapiganapo tempo, nyasi huu mia!). Put another way, the painful experience of the Byaruhanga family in exile is a reminder to all reasonable and moral people that "war has no eyes."

In the fall of 1983, Mary received a message from a traveler that her husband was, indeed, alive and had been seen in a refugee camp in

Burundi. Her immediate response was predictably jubilance. With laughter and with tears of joy pouring from her eyes, all Mary could say was, "Praise God! Praise God! Praise God my husband is alive!" A religious organization in Nairobi, the All African Conference of Churches, assisted in reuniting the entire Byaruhanga family that fall.

By this point in our conversation, a mix of joy and sorrow, pain and promise, rage and awe, and hope and despair filled the room. It was, for me, a moment of genuine renewal and unabashed hope in the freeing and unfailing promises of God! In the splendor of this fleeting moment, I stopped being an interviewer and became one with them in celebration of the mighty acts of God. As a person of faith, I could not help but wonder, Why has God entrusted, to such frail human vessels, the precious cargo of the gospel of Jesus Christ? Without doubt, there is a glorious mystery in our personal journeys of faith that defies both formal structures of logic and the canons of systematic theology. I next inquired, "How did you endure the pain of separation as a divided refugee family?"

CHARLES: I had a lot of doubts and bad feelings running around in my head at first. . . . Then I prayed to God, and, strangely, I remembered my vows of baptism when I was a child.

INTERVIEWER: Baptism?

CHARLES: Yes, I do mean baptism . . . You see, baptism in my own village was not an individual act or anything like that; it was a community event, a festive sharing and celebration by the villagers . . . Many were poor but happy people. All the time when I was at the refugee camp in Burundi I felt inside that somebody else was sharing in my burden.

MARY: All the while the family was apart, I had my moments of doubt but I never completely lost hope.

INTERVIEWER: What do you mean?

MARY: I mean faith can do wonders.

CHARLES: Yes! I think we mean almost the same thing—faith is *real*. All I thought about was my family and someday being reunited with Mary, Juliet, Julius, Jane, Sarah, and my son, Solomon.

INTERVIEWER: Will you say more about faith experiences as a refugee family?

CHARLES: Well, we still have our struggles and problems. We still are refugees living in exile from home . . . We are worried and distressed because we can't go home, at least not right now with things being the way they are in Uganda. I feel that I'm still in danger and would be picked up if I tried now to take my family back. What am I to do? I can't go back, and I don't feel at real ease or that happy here. Kenya is not our home.

INTERVIEWER: But what about your faith?

CHARLES: Sure, we both have faith, don't misunderstand me . . . There are things that bother me and I don't really know what's going to happen to us as refugees. But faith—I do have faith. It was faith that helped me get into school and pass my exams, and it was faith that brought my family back to me.

MARY: I'm not much with words, but I know this—we are alive today because of faith. We are alive today by trusting in God; and even now the St. Paul's community helps us and the children.

INTERVIEWER: What have you learned about suffering in your exile?

CHARLES: For one thing, by suffering I've learned how to survive . . . Suffering teaches us how to survive. It lets you know that you can do with little things, when you used to have a lot. And I trust more in God now, because of my troubles and sufferings. I read my Bible more. I found in the letter of Peter something that really struck home with me: "For one is approved if, mindful of God, he endures pain while suffering unjustly. For what credit is it, if when you do wrong and are beaten for it you take it patiently? But if when you do right and suffer for it you take it patiently, you have God's approval" (1 Peter 2:20).

Mary had no response, only silence. She appeared to feel many emotions inside her very soul. A few minutes later she regained her composure and said, "As a Christian, what suffering and being in exile has taught me is how to be patient. I didn't know the meaning of patience at home . . . I took life for granted, because we had everything. Now we have nothing—nothing but each other and God. So what I have learned through suffering is how to be simple, really simple about the basics of life, because the life of a refugee is very hard."

Suddenly, with unexpected energy, Mary and Charles began to share further, from the depth of their souls, what being a refugee is really like. For them, being a refugee means finding yourself in a place where you feel you don't belong; eating food that tastes strange; drinking water that you can barely swallow; sleeping on the ground in a mud hut instead of a bed—or not sleeping at all; talking to people, but not being understood because of language barriers; praying to a God in a strange land and wondering if your prayers are being heard. A refugee is a homeless, jobless, landless, countryless peasant. Ironic as it is tragic, century-old traditions that once gave stability to life and family instantly disappear among refugees. Many refugees live a suspended existence, having lost control over their own destiny. Over 7 million refugees in Africa aimlessly roam from one border camp to another, seeking whatever they can find to survive. Words such as "dignity" and "self-respect" have no meaning when a person is hungry or thirsty—all you want at that moment is food and water! The only way for this to stop is to go home—the hope of *homecoming*! But for Charles and Mary Byaruhanga and their five children, that hope is still a dream.

In the uneven rhythm of their own exile, the family is painfully aware that there are no guarantees for the future when you live the life of a perpetual wanderer. Speaking for countless refugees in Kenya and Uganda, Charles and Mary reminded me of the chilling presence of *uncertainty*. An agonizing uncertainty that cracks people's emotions as they move from one place to another in search of water, food, and shelter. Charles put it this way: "You know that tomorrow will be just like today . . . For the refugee, you know that life becomes a life of line ups . . . You line up for water; you line up for food, you line up for shots; you line up for ID registration; you line up for messages about missing relatives . . . You line up for the graveyard."

In terms of a wider view on the refugee problem, it is important to point out that the precarious life of the Byaruhanga family is one grain of sand upon a vast stormy beach. They are not alone. Their experience represents three facts of refugee life in certain African countries today: (1) nobody chooses to be a refugee; (2) these exiles are largely victims of political, economic, and military realities within their own countries; they have no choice but to run brave and hard in order to survive and to save the lives of their families; (3) we all are *potential* refugees in our global village!

Thousands of Ugandan refugee families participate daily in the ritual of "waiting and hoping" to cross the borders of Kenya, southern Sudan, or other countries in search of the survival-essentials. Their perennial search is for peace and security in countries where there is neither peace nor security—only revolving doors. The Byaruhanga family was among the "lucky" ones, or they were blessed by God, for at least they got out with their lives. This alone is no small miracle of faith. Therefore, it would be difficult to convince Charles and Mary that the mighty hand of God was not "there-in-the-shadow-of-exile-experience," and that God was not a faithful watchman in the night.

The Byaruhanga family is still living in exile on the campus of St. Paul's

United Theological College, Limuru, Kenya. Charles is enrolled in University College, an area technical school, where he is studying accounting. Student life has been difficult for him as a husband and father. Stubbornly persistent and hopeful, Charles is in school six days per week, with a total of twenty-eight class periods to be attended from Monday through Saturday. Mary is busy learning new skills in the art of weaving. They receive a total subsidy of only 900 shillings per month from the All Africa Conference of Churches, and Mary sells her handcrafts to supplement the family income.

The Byaruhangas' single goal for the future is also their dilemma: Will they be able to return to Uganda? Can homecoming be a reality, or is it a mere hope? Will it be a time of celebration or lamentation? After nine agonizing years in exile, Charles and Mary are visibly troubled and wonder if they will be gone for another nine. For both of them, the issue of exile appears to be not a question of having more faith or less faith, but a question of belonging. As the winds of change blow fiercely across Africa, they wonder to which future they belong. At the close of our conversation, Charles confessed and lamented, "There is a strange feeling inside . . . that you do not belong to where you are, and you can't be where you belong."

DISCUSSION NOTES

The wider question of the refugee problem in Africa is depicted and highlighted in the painful story of Charles and Mary Byaruhanga. The political scandal of the refugee problem offends the moral sensibility of most human beings in our society and around the world. It would be hypocritical for middle-class North American Christians—black or white—to pretend they know what it is like to suffer the abject poverty and pain of an African refugee family. To do so, in my opinion, would be self-righteous and arrogant.

For the Christian community, what is at stake in this case involving the lives of Charles, Mary, and their five children are the issues of (1) our moral openness to enter the cycle of pain of a family desperately struggling to survive and stay together; and (2) how God figures at the center of this equation.

Perhaps yet another issue to be addressed in this case, by all of us, is the nature of Christian faith in the African context. In Africa, Christian faith is not first and foremost intellectual knowledge or inquiries about biblical doctrine and church history. Nor is it knowledge for the mere pursuit of knowledge. Rather as with Charles and Mary, faith is more an anchor for survival in a hostile world than a tool of inquiry about universal truth. Charles, more vocal than Mary, expressed the feeling that many Western missionaries taught the idea of faith as a type of knowledge to be mastered, over against the basic invitation of Jesus Christ to love one another and to do justice. For the Byaruhanga family, this would be an intellectual error and would be unnatural and foreign to genuine African Christianity and culture.

This case may give us a better understanding of the complexity of the refugee problem in our world community. To be sure, the refugee problem is often made worse by government and military corruption and cruelty, which innocent and homeless people must suffer. I am still haunted by the sharp whisper of Charles's voice in my ear:

> Nobody chooses to be a refugee . . . We are victims of a bad political situation . . . We are scared. We run with the wind to survive, and only God knows where the wind is going.

Remembering the biblical images of the Holy Spirit and the particular focus in Old Testament literature on the *ruah* (the Spirit, or "Eastwind," of God), maybe the clues in this case can help in the discussion of the faith stories of Charles and Mary Byaruhanga. To assist in the methodological dialogue, we may consider some issues and questions.

Ethical Approach

1. How would you go about informing people in your church or community about the refugee problem in Africa or the problem of the homeless in the United States?
2. What sort of moral directions do we find in the Bible regarding the plight of the homeless ones?
3. How can local churches assist in responding to the critical needs of refugees?

Issues for Reflection

1. What issues are at stake in this case?
2. Where do you begin?
3. How would you likely respond to the moral dilemma and immediate problems facing Charles and Mary?
4. With the rapid increase in the world refugee problem, what options do we have in the future?

SUGGESTED READING

Beckmann, David, and Elizabeth Anne Donnelly. *The Overseas List: Opportunities for Living and Working in Developing Countries.* Minneapolis: Augsburg Publishing House, 1979.

Casa Haliga, Pedro. *I Believe in Justice and Hope.* Notre Dame, Ind.: Fides/Claretian, 1978.

de Gruchy, John. *Cry Justice.* Maryknoll, N.Y.: Orbis Books, 1986.

Evans, Alice F., Robert A. Evans, and W. B. Kennedy. *Pedagogies for the Non-Poor.* Maryknoll, N.Y.: Orbis Books, 1987.

Gremillion, Joseph, and William Ryan, eds. *World Faiths and the New World Order.* Interreligious Peace Colloquium, 3700 13th Street, N.E., Washington, D.C. 20017.

Koyama, Kosuke. *Three Mile an Hour God.* Maryknoll, N.Y.: Orbis Books, 1979.

Ngugi, James. *Weep Not, Child.* Nairobi, Kenya: General Printers, 1984.

Ngugi, Wa Thiong'o. *Homecoming.* Nairobi, Kenya: Heinemann Educational Books, 1972.

Simon, Arthur. *Bread for the World.* New York: Paulist Press; Grand Rapids: Wm. B. Eerdmans, 1975.

Taylor, John V. *Enough Is Enough.* Minneapolis: Augsburg Publishing House, 1977.

CASE
2
THE MAU MAU CHAPLAIN

This case arises from the experiences, struggles, and hopes of an African lay theologian whose life and faith journeys were shaped during and by a critical period in Kenyan history known as the Mau Mau.[1] Peter K. Njoroge is forty-six years old. He is one of the elder sons born to Njoroge Wathuku and Alice Muthoni. A robust child raised in a polygamous household, Peter actually referred to "home" as a place of two mothers—his natural biological mother and Paulina Nyokabi, his *maitu munjinji*, or junior mother. A man of medium build with gentle but stoic features, Peter seems to command the ground upon which he walks. Spontaneous and warm, even at first glance he is revealed as a man burning with the fire of faith, courage, and passion for a community whose God is not alien to African soil. Moreover, one can observe in Peter Njoroge a restless passion as he spoke candidly of "we," "our struggle," "our vision." This mode of speech was present throughout our conversation about his self-understanding of faith and liberation.

As we sat in the solitude of my makeshift study in Limuru, I was surprised, as a case writer, by Peter's perpetual warmth and frankness. Peter is the sort of man with a positive view of the future—despite the suffering and pain in African society—and a burning faith in God and that people can make a difference.

Peter is happily married to Sophia Wambui Kairie, and they are the proud parents of eight children, Paul Njoroge, John Bosco Karanja, Carolina Muthoni, Elizabeth Njeri, Cecilia Waithera, Francisca Mukami, Maria Regina Wanjiku, and Esther Clar Wanjiu. With spirit and good humor, Peter affectionately referred to his family as "my small domestic church," the place where things come together for the average African.

Peter grew up in a small village community in the Kiambu District of the central province of Kenya. The people of his village practiced a form of communal living where individual families shared responsibilities in cultivating crops for the local market. Peter referred to this form of interaction as "African-grassroot-socialism." His childhood community was, therefore, a place where nobody—friend, neighbor, or stranger—lived outside the economy of the family. Seasonal work on the land—which involved planting and harvesting corn, sugar cane, coffee, tea, and other crops—reflected the spirit of community and the principle of mutuality among the Kikuyu people.

Peter K. Njoroge was fortunate and attended the Queen of Apostle Seminary, where he received his high school diploma in the late 1950s. In 1958, Peter's faith pilgrimage took a decisive turn. Because of his desire for more education, he enrolled as a student studying for the priesthood at the Moroguro Seminary in the neighboring country of Tanzania. Peter was banned from acquiring advanced education in Kenya because he was regarded by some as a political agitator against British colonial rule at the time. He was forced into exile in order to continue his theological studies. While a student at Moroguro Seminary for four years, Peter concentrated his studies in philosophy and theology. He had a keen interest in the implications of these disciplines for his own work and ministry with people victimized by colonial rule.

There is in indigenous African literature a proverb which says, "A spider's web united can tie up a lion." Increasingly in Peter's judgment and faith struggles, African Kenyan peasants were beginning to unite—fueled by the fire of independence and Mau Mau revolutionaries—and to work against the "lion" of British colonialism in the name of a God of justice. A pivotal turning point in his seminary years, an event that led to his expulsion, was an assignment to write a critique of the biblical term "prophet" and to apply it to a contemporary leader or figure. The year was 1962, and Peter was near the end of his theological study at Moroguro. In his paper, focused on a biblical critique of Jomo Kenyatta as social prophet. Peter K. Njoroge wrote,

> To be God's prophet includes that, first, you are really sent by God and get a message from Him. Secondly, you actually teach or speak the message you were given faithfully . . . the primary duty of the prophet is to teach those things which God has revealed to him, faithfully . . . When people call Jomo Kenyatta or Gandhi a prophet, the concept of prophet is analogically used. People see a person like Jomo to be God-raised to speak, teach and fight for African nationalism. Since the dignity and freedom of man is God-

given, such a man teaches what is a datum of creation whose author is God
. . . People see them [prophets] as God-sent to free them from their
oppression.

In the political and moral climate in Africa today, this sort of biblical
interpretation by an African student of theology would probably go
unnoticed; it would certainly be unlikely that such a statement would
result in dismissal. But in the African political climate of 1962, this
responsive statement was considered radical and subversive. Suddenly
Peter, a promising young candidate for the priesthood, found himself
expelled from the degree program at Moroguro Seminary. According to
Peter, the school did not publicly announce or make official the "reasons" behind its action, but nearly everybody in the seminary community
knew exactly what had happened. From this event in his pilgrimage and
faith struggle, Peter was dubbed by friend and foe alike the "Mau Mau
Chaplain." This crisis in Peter's life marked the end of his formal
education. Yet for the past twenty-six years, Peter has continued self-
directed study and research on the impact of Christianity on Kenyan
culture. He works as a lay Catholic theologian and activist in Kenya.

A brief glimpse into the formative years of this "African priest"
suggests that Peter ran hard against the winds of colonial domination and
exploitation. His identity and social consciousness were shaped in the
late 1940s and early 1950s by the spirit of independence and revolutionary
nationalism that swept across many African countries. The Mau Mau
movement had enormous impact on Kenyan history and the struggle for
independence, especially during the 1950s. And Peter's childhood and
identity, his passion and agitation for social justice can be adequately
understood only by understanding this sociohistorical period.

Peter's character and early faith experience were deeply influenced by
his grandfather, Thyuku Njoroge, his biological mother, Alice Muthoni,
and his father, Njoro Wa Thuku. In our conversations, he constantly
referred to his grandfather as a *Muthamakai Njamba* (meaning in the
Kikuyu vernacular "grave patriot" or "great man of faith"). As an
esteemed elder of the community, grandpa Njoroge taught young Peter
and others the value of tradition and respect for their religious symbols,
rites, and customs. "I remember that grandpa wore with pride the old
dress and costumes and symbols of our people," explained Peter.

What appears to stand out most about his mother during the formative
years was the fun they shared around the fireplace—usually right before
evening meal time when they would sing traditional songs and listen to
the elders tell stories and fables.

For Peter, storytelling and religion form the dynamic center of African communal life. Indeed, religion, he feels, gives life. Peter recalled a favorite song of his childhood. In the rhythmic form of the oral tradition, one stanza went like this:

O little children, O little children,
Pray ye truly, pray ye honestly;
For God is the same God for
All eternity!

While he was growing up, then, expressions of faith and storytelling filled village life. Peter vividly remembered certain religious precepts and principles laid down by his father which impacted his own character. He shared one example of what his father told his sons and daughters: "First, God hates no one. Second, the one hated by people is not necessarily hated by God. Third, the one who oppresses the poor will not prevent the sun from rising. Fourth, God's fire is kept alive through the night with banana fibers. Fifth, remember my children that when the truth strikes, it breaks the bow. Sixth, a homestead is in greatest danger when the warriors grow up." This last saying was particularly relevant to Peter's growing self-understanding in that it served, in his words, "to warn parents to take care of the children in the home and to encourage our young ones to grow up to care for the land and village life." These sayings were the moral fiber which held together the Njoroge family during the difficult years of the Kenyan struggle for independence. In one sense, the story of Peter, the acclaimed Mau Mau chaplain, is a microcosm of the wider movement of conscience of Kenyan peasants in the mid-1950s, who were passionately struggling for a new dignity and a place to hang their hats in the homeland of their ancestors.

In the course of our conversation on the themes of faith and liberation, I was amazed to discover the "literal concreteness" with which Peter spoke about these matters. A strong belief inherent in the tradition of Kikuyu people is God's immanence, the idea that God intervenes in the concrete problems, struggles, and affairs of oppressed people. For Peter, faith in a God of immanence is critical when confronting a crisis of any kind. "Faith is not abstract," exclaimed Peter, "but something that meets us on the perilous roads of life . . . Faith in this kind of God helps us not to panic in different situations." As an example, Peter related to me an experience he had as a young man in his village community. One day he and a group of friends went into a restricted area of the forest to play. Soon they were laughing and full of merrymaking. Suddenly they heard a loud rumbling noise in the bush, and a pack of rhinoceros came charging their way! Two of his friends panicked and became hysterical—but fortunately they all managed to escape by climbing a tree until help arrived. Though subdued and shaken by this ordeal, Peter later realized that he was the only one who had not panicked. He attributed this to what he called the "miracle of faith" and his strong belief that God actually intervenes to deliver people—both sinners and saints—from danger and death.

I then posed the question, "How do you account for such faith in a situation of danger or crisis?" Reflecting on the seriousness of my question, Peter responded, "You know, my grandpa was a traditional Kikuyu elder, a great man of faith. Times were very hard in my village when I was a child, and I remember grandpa quoting from the Bible, from Hebrews where it said, 'Now faith is the substance of things hoped for' . . . It seemed that the only thought we had then was our hope for independence. Despite the suffering of my people, that was the one thing we all 'hoped for.' For us colonialism was our great time of crisis, and faith helped us to deal with it and be victorious . . . It helped us to struggle for freedom and justice; and the thing about grandpa was that he made us see the strength of faith in our own traditional beliefs."

It became increasingly clear to me as Peter unraveled the fabric of his story that faith for him was something more than a word; it was a deep sense of reverence for God. He feels that God sees us through crisis—cleansing, renewing, and restoring lives shattered by oppression and sin. Faith itself is by no means purely personal. In traditional Kikuyu culture, the idea of faith was always understood in a social sense. "I get disturbed easily by the term 'personal,' " confessed Peter, "for our way of seeing faith is not personal but communal . . . As I struggled and worked for justice back then, I was not alone; my mother was there, my father was there, my brother was there . . . The spirit of the ancestors is always there."

Peter then spoke about the two sides of faith in the Kikuyu cultural and religious tradition: the spiritual being of faith and the physical being of faith. In both, Peter believed that the reality of faith amidst the uncertain throes of life enables the Christian to endure. The seeds of liberation and the thirst for truth, under the Lordship of Christ, appear to be deeply embedded in Peter's spiritual life. Over the last twenty-five years of his social ministry as a lay theologian and activist, Peter has lived out of the pain and promise of his own convictions about God and Jesus Christ. He has felt the need to proclaim the gospel but in his own way and faithful to his sense of calling. In a widely circulated Catholic newsletter entitled, "Voices From the Pew" (1961), Peter the Mau Mau chaplain had these words to say regarding the mission of the church in Africa:

> Above all Christ is the Preacher of good tidings to enslaved and unhappy mankind. He preaches, "my burden is light and my yoke is sweet." Christ has an all-consuming love for mankind whence his reverence, adaptation, and reasonableness to all men.

Coming from a young, developing Christian living on the eve of Kenyan independence from British colonial rule, this was quite a remarkable expression of faith in a Christ who sides with the "enslaved and the oppressed." In the course of our conversation, Peter K. Njoroge consistently expressed the view that God in Christ was the "liberating force" behind the Kenyan struggle for independence and the right to self-determination. As Mau Mau chaplain, Peter understood Christianity as grounded in a liberation-experience, especially his reading of the exodus story and the narrative teachings of Jesus. Peter's theological view is that this deeper struggle for truth and dignity ultimately led the Kenyan peasantry to resist oppression and to win their freedom in the early 1960s. The Kikuyu have a proverb which expresses this sentiment: "He who is driven away by a club returns, but he who is driven away by truth does not return." Hence, in Peter's own pilgrimage of faith the "truth" and rightness of the Kenyan cause for freedom was the decisive force that drove out the colonizers. In short, truth resists all forms of oppression and demoralization.

But near the close of the interview, it became clear that despite the various ways in which Peter himself has struggled to maintain courage, there still remains in his own mind the unresolved problems of neocolonialism and concern about the current plight of the poor under African political leadership. At the practical daily level, what seems to bother Peter a great deal in his continuing journey of faith is that young Africans now appear to be losing ground, with respect to upholding traditional values and identity. Perhaps here the more intriguing question is Why?

DISCUSSION NOTES

This case, in part, provides us with a glimpse into the life of a courageous African Christian who has been deeply affected by the residual effects of British colonialism and by the hope of freedom. Peter K. Njoroge is a person of unusual spiritual stamina and faith.

There are three main points in this case:

1. The rhythmic flow of Njoroge's faith pilgrimage leads us to read the gospel of Jesus Christ as a messianic story concerned with the liberation of Kenyan people in (and not from) history.
2. Peter's painful sense of abandonment after expulsion from seminary may open real opportunities for hope and the renewal of faith as North American Christians consider their own moments of abandonment and vulnerability.
3. The drama of Njoroge's case may challenge the contemporary Western church to understand better the contextualization of Christian faith. The gospel of Jesus Christ must be both particular and universal in speaking to human suffering and oppression.

In a broader sense, this case may also offer an understanding of the complex social and political problems of a country groping for more direction on the eve of independence from British colonial rule. As an African Christian seeking to make sense out of his oppressed condition and calling, Peter Njoroge consistently expresses the view that God sides with the marginalized and hurting ones in our world. In his social perception of reality, the dominant image of God in village and communal life is one of Liberator. For him, the image of God-in-Christ is that of a liberation-force.

Discussion participants may wish to highlight the parallels here with the biblical views of God not only as Liberator of Israel from the bondage of death and oppression in Egypt, but also as Sustainer of new life. In terms of Kenyan history, Peter K. Njoroge rightly understands the exodus story as a liberation event—the struggle by poor and destitute Kenyans to win their independence and dignity in the early 1960s from British rule and domination. While the larger question of liberation is obviously dominant in this case, the themes of identity, cultural integrity, and hope for a better future in Kikuyu society are also powerfully represented in the life and faith journeys of Peter K. Njoroge. Can his personal struggle, hopes, and cultural situation contribute to our understanding of how the Christian gospel should be lived in the world?

Other issues that can be a beginning point for small group discussion include faith as life-giving, the interface of "folk wisdom and justice" in old village culture, the value of the extended family tradition, and the idea of God as one who sides with the poor and the oppressed. Individuals make moral choices that affect their lives each day. We may then ask in this case, How can Christians make the choices that are biblically faithful and ethically freeing? In terms of his inclinations for theological training, did Peter Njoroge's situation merit expulsion from seminary? Imagine yourself a seminary classmate of Peter's. What advice or feelings would you share regarding Christ as "preacher of good tidings to the enslaved"? We may further wish to approach this case by disciplined reflection on the following questions and concerns.

NOTES

1. The *Mau Mau* may be described as a revolutionary nationalist movement against British colonial domination and oppression, on the part of Kenyan Africans in their struggle for freedom and the right to self-determination. Writers and scholars describe the Mau Mau period in various ways. Some argue that the Mau Mau period began when the first European settlers came to the country; others are more attentive to the historical period immediately before 1952 and then the period of Emergency. Kenya won its independence in 1963. According to the Kenyan writer Ngugi: "The basic objectives of Mau Mau revolutionaries were to drive out the Europeans, seize the government, and give back to the Kenya peasants their stolen lands and property." See Wa Thiong'o Ngugi, *Homecoming* (Nairobi: Heinemann Educational Books, 1972), 28. For further study on Mau Mau, see Donald L. Barrett and Karari Njama, *Mau Mau from Within*, (London: MacGibbon & Kee, 1966); Carl G. Rosberg and John Nottingham, *The Myth of Mau Mau*, (Nairobi: East Africa Publishing House, 1966); and David W. Throup, *Economic and Social Origins of Mau Mau*, 1943–53 (Nairobi: Heinemann Educational Books, 1988).

Ethical Approach

1. How would you likely respond to Peter's internal struggle and expulsion from the seminary?
2. What is the role of faith in a crisis situation?
3. What parallels, if any, do you see between certain African sayings or proverbs and those in your own cultural setting?

Issues for Reflection

1. What are the relevant issues or problems at stake in this case?
2. What do you think of Peter's theological view that God sides with the oppressed?
3. What is the meaning of Christian faith for people who suffer?

SUGGESTED READING

Aluko, Olajide, ed. *The Foreign Policies of African States*. London: Hodder & Stoughton; Atlantic Highlands, N.J.: Humanities, 1977.

Armah, Ayi Kwei. *The Beautiful Ones Are Not Yet Born*. Boston: Houghton Mifflin, 1968; London: Heinemann Educational Books, 1969.

———. *Two Thousand Seasons*. Nairobi, Kenya: East African Publishing House, 1973.

Essien-Udom, Essien Udosen. *Black Nationalism*. Chicago: University of Chicago Press, 1962.

Hastings, Adrian. *A History of African Christianity 1950–75*. Cambridge and New York: Cambridge University Press, 1979.

Kenyatta, Jomo. *Facing Mount Kenya: The Tribal Life of the Kikuyu, 1938*. London and Nairobi: Heinemann Educational Books, 1971; New York: AMS Press, 1978.

Mazrui, Ali Al'Amin. *The African: A Triple Heritage*. Boston: Little, Brown & Co., 1986.

———. *World Culture and the Black Experience*. Seattle: University of Washington Press, 1974.

Mazrui, Ali Al'Amin, and M. Tidy. *Nationalism and New States in Africa from About 1935 to the Present*. London and Portsmouth, N.H.: Heinemann Educational Books, 1984.

Throup, David W. *Economic and Social Origins of Mau Mau, 1945–53*. Nairobi, Kenya: Heinemann Educational Books, 1988.

CASE
3

CONFESSIONS OF A
WOMANIST WOMAN

"A woman's place is in the home—not the seminary," quipped Nathan Mworia, chairman of the admissions committee of St. James Theological College, Nairobi, Kenya. Mr. Mworia has been chair of the powerful admissions committee for the last eight years. Prior to that, he served for two years as the top administrative assistant to the chancellor of the seminary, Rev. Dr. Arthur Solamei, a respected leader and educator in local church and community circles. The history of this theological college stretches back to the days of colonialism in eastern Africa. Though conservative in its theological doctrines, the school is proud of its diverse heritage and traditions, and its ecumenical roots. St. James is interdenominational in character and was founded by church leaders from the Baptist, Methodist, and East African Pentecostal churches. Its purpose was to equip pastors and lay people for the work of Christian ministry in Kenya.

Since St. James Theological College opened in 1959, its philosophy has been one of total commitment to the training of men for Christian service in response to the spiritual hunger of a growing population which is increasingly urban in outlook and value-orientation. Perhaps of particular note is the fact that the Baptists came to this region in 1956, when the Foreign Mission Board in America sent missionaries along with their families to witness to the gospel of Jesus Christ. St. James has a faculty of ten fulltime members and six parttime, and an assortment of church connections and organizational affiliations. The seminary is often looked to by the community for leadership, especially in the area of lay theological education. The school has approximately seventy-five students, all male.

Although there are no bylaws in the school's charter that prohibit women from admission to the degree program, custom has disfavored the presence of women students in the seminary community. Insiders would testify that all of this is a matter of record, but it was perhaps one of the school's best kept secrets until Rosemary Otunga appeared on the seminary scene. Rosemary was not the first woman to apply for admission to St. James. Two women had earlier been admitted to the regular degree program but neither had finished the course of study.

A single woman, Rosemary is twenty-four years old and a Baptist. She hails from the township of Kakamega, in western Kenya, and is by tribe or kinship system Kikuyu. Rosemary had applied for admission two previous times; each time her application was flatly rejected by Mr. Mworia's committee on the grounds that the candidate's vocational views appeared to be "incompatible with the essential theological affirmations of the school."

Rosemary's academic records indicated that she is a person of intellectual ability and maturity. She finished Form Four and has the Western equivalent of a high school diploma. This level of educational achievement normally qualifies a candidate for admission when accompanied by proper recommendations—which Rosemary had. A former member of the youth fellowship and an active participant in her local church, Rosemary comes from a strong Christian family. She has four sisters and three older brothers. For the most part, Rosemary's immediate family is supportive of her decision for ministry.

Rosemary's story of personal faith is of a person caught up in the crosscurrents of a changing society, as African women seek a new identity—one that is often in tension and conflict with traditional customs and beliefs.

As an interviewer and faith-partner, I asked, "Rosemary, what prompted you to attend seminary?" She replied, "Why not seminary? I felt God was leading me into the work of ministry. God created all of us in God's image, male and female, and God delights and takes pleasure in each woman—just like man . . . Isn't the image of God planted in woman too?"

Without giving me a chance to respond to her rhetorical question, she continued, "Many women in our culture do important things, but don't get much credit for them . . . Most men seem to feel that the only thing a woman is good for is in the home, in the kitchen, in the bedroom, or working on the *shamba* and raising children . . . Now, is it wrong for me to think that a woman's shadow should extend beyond these things, however they are? I do deeply believe that God uses both men and women in all of God's vineyard. I feel the call of God . . ."

I probed further, "What do you mean by call?" In reply Rosemary said, "To be honest, I'm not sure about what it all really means; I have questions and doubts . . . I do think this is why I felt a need to come to seminary and perhaps get some answers. Prior to seminary, I did learn, however, that God used many women in biblical times for the good of the people of faith. I recall my Sunday school teacher mentioning Miriam, who led a nation's women to praise the Lord; I recall Hulda, a woman who revealed God's plans to national leaders; Ruth and Sarah, who were examples of faithfulness in covenant relationships; Hannah, the ideal mother; Esther, who risked her own life to serve God's people. Are we to say that a person who desires to grow spiritually should be excluded because of sex? I feel that was a factor in my struggle for and the denial of my admission here at St. James."

For reasons not fully known, after her third attempt, Rosemary was in fact admitted to the regular degree program of the seminary. And through much toil, personal struggle, discipline, and encouragement from the people of the community, she eventually graduated. But there is more to this unfolding drama of faith.

Our conversation about her faith journey took place shortly after her graduation. She told me that not long after her application was rejected the second time by the admissions committee, she had slipped into a deep state of depression and frustration, as feelings of self-doubt and failure grew. In her own despair, Rosemary confessed, "I was near the edge, my emotions and feelings had been hit with a cold, wet blanket; I even questioned my call from the Lord . . . That was a difficult time for me, and it seemed that nothing was going right, despite all my efforts to prove myself and my worth at St. James." Rosemary bitterly lamented, "I had about given up—except for the grace of God!"

As she continued to tell me about her faith struggles and doubts, I could not help but observe the tension in Rosemary's voice and the look of anguish on her face. As one called to the ministry of Christ, she had apparently experienced more than her share of pain and rejection—and little support except from family and close friends in her own church community. In another conversation, Rosemary admitted feeling depression and abandonment, anxiety and guilt over her "womanist" reality in seminary. For Rosemary, seminary education was a goal worth fighting for, but the mixed feelings and doubt remained. Then a strange thing happened. Rosemary went on a three-day fast of prayer and meditation, seeking spiritual strength and guidance from the Lord God. A traditional Kikuyu custom is the belief that genuine fasting has three requirements of the aspirant: (1) the person fasting must be under the spiritual guidance of a senior elder (*gethuuri* or *kamatimo*, elders of lesser grade), or what is called a "spiritual director" in some traditions of Western Christianity; (2) the aspirant must wear a long pair of white socks but no sandals or shoes; and (3) the elder of the community must escort the aspirant to a designated large oak tree in the valley at the river bank, where they offer prayers facing Mount Kenya. Rosemary completed this exercise of spiritual discipline and, as if miraculously, not many days later was actually admitted to the seminary community. Rosemary vividly recalls the first words that fell from her lips on the day of her acceptance: "Praise the Lord. Halleluia!" "Praise the Lord. Halleluia!!!" The majestic sound of these words still looms large in her heart and soul three years later.

As a woman of faith, Rosemary's spiritual and practical devotion to God appear to permeate her relationships with others—although the pain of her womanist reality cannot be easily covered over. As for the ministry as vocation, Rosemary feels that every woman has her own special gift from God. Self-discovery is therefore the moral burden of each living soul. Each has a unique personality: "Each is an example of God's creativity," says Rosemary.

While as a woman of faith Rosemary has many role models, the biblical character who seems to stand out in her own mind is Esther. She tends to identify with Esther from a vocational perspective because in her own view, Esther was not afraid to face difficult situations: "I and my maids will also fast as you do. Then I will go to the king, though it is against the law; and if I perish, I perish" (Est. 4:16).

Rosemary's seminary experience was not, by any stretch of the imagination, easy. There were difficult days and worrisome nights, as papers and required reading piled up. She tells of a professor who had problems with the idea of ordaining women for Christian ministry. He taught Old Testament theology and invariably found subtle ways to make discouraging and sexist comments about the quality of her work. One day after class, Rosemary confronted him in a manner that was respectful but firm. She said, "I'm a Christian like everyone else in this class, and I don't particularly know your real feelings toward me and my work; but this I do know, I only want fairness . . . in the grading of the work I turn in; I'm not looking for a handout—only fairness."

Of course there were teachers and colleagues more ethically sensitive who gave Rosemary encouragement and hope as a woman in ministry.

She recalled a rather interesting incident during the "make-you, break-you" first semester of seminary life. With hope beaming from her face, Rosemary recalled these words spoken by her orientation teacher: "You come to seminary not to memorize sound doctrines or to quote scriptures better than another, but to get your guts torn out. But be not dismayed: Jesus is the master surgeon!" For Rosemary, these words stood out like thorns amidst roses during her bittersweet journey through seminary.

With graduation behind her and the future ahead, Rosemary wonders about the thorns yet to be confronted in her own church. She has not yet found placement in her own village community of Kakamega, on the western plains of Kenya.

DISCUSSION NOTES

By American standards of social morality, this is not a simple case of sexism involving the life and struggles of Rosemary Otunga, a young African woman in pursuit of the ministry. It is not primarily a case about African religious traditionalism over against Western values aimed at assessing the relative progress women have made, given the various career options in church and society today. It is not primarily a case about dominance of African men over African women. The issues of this case are far more subtle. They are integral to our basic perceptions and worldview. They are integral to our web of social experience. They are integral to our view of God as a shaping force in the Christian moral life.

Rosemary's case is a profile in courage, the courage of a radical faith that believes that each woman is created by God equal and full. From an Afro-centric perspective, all moral claims are subject to debate, including the moral claim or belief that human worth and equality cannot be determined, either on the basis of individual production in the market-place or the social forces of gender and tribe in village life.

For theological discussion, the issue at stake in the case is not purely one of the "place" of women in traditional African society, but also the meaning of the faith Rosemary, as a child of God, has in "womanist reality." Novelist Alice Walker has described emerging black feminism— whether in Africa or North America—as "womanist." The term "womanist," I suspect, may be used in group discussion to capture the essence of what it means to be *woman, Christian*, and *African*, as well as a contemplative human being who struggles with life and death issues between the poles of experience and expectation.

Further, one may wish to explore in this case the phenomenon of "womanist reality" to test our thoughts and impressions as to whether there is a universal experience for women seminarians. While it is difficult to predict whether this sort of approach to case dialogue will yield new insight—given the tensions between African culture and Euro-American culture—nonetheless, it is worth serious ethical consideration. In reflection upon the term "womanist reality," one is struck by the fact that women graduates of seminaries often tell of similar experiences: (1) morally ungrounded suspicion by male seminarians of women's real motive for theological study; (2) loneliness and hidden frustration within the seminary environment; (3) competition for top grades; and (4) the "superwoman syndrome." In short, it is not hard to understand some of the difficulties experienced by Rosemary in response to her own call and her passionate quest for theological training for the furtherance of the gospel.

Who should decide the right of theological passage?

Ethical Approach

1. How would you respond to Rosemary Otunga's dilemma?
2. What biblical resources would you draw upon to affirm or deny ordination for women?
3. List at least three ways the seminary community of St. James may better confront the issues of sexism and male dominance?

Issues for Reflection

1. What are the main issues at stake in this case?
2. What role does tradition play in shaping one's social attitudes toward women?
3. Who did Jesus call to be "bearers" or "proclaimers" of the good news?

SUGGESTED READING

Carmody, Denise L. *Biblical Women: Contemporary Reflections on Scriptural Texts.* New York: Crossroad, 1988.

Faxon, Alicia Craig. *Women and Jesus.* Philadelphia: United Church Press, 1973.

Gundry, Patricia. *Women Be Free! Free to Be God's Woman.* Grand Rapids: Zondervan Publishing House, 1979.

Nouwen, Henri. *Creative Ministry.* New York: Doubleday & Co., 1971.

Ochs, Carol. *Behind the Sex of God.* Boston: Beacon Press, 1977.

Ochshorn, Judith. *The Female Experience and the Nature of the Divine.* Bloomington: Indiana University Press, 1980.

O'Faolain, Julia, and Lauro Martines, eds. *Not in God's Image*. New York: Harper & Row, 1973.

Otwell, John H. *And Sarah Laughed: The Status of Woman in the Old Testament*. Philadelphia: Westminster Press, 1977.

Paton, David M., ed. *Breaking Barriers: The Report of the Fifth Assembly of the World Council of Churches, Nairobi, 1975*. Grand Rapids: Wm. B. Eerdmans, 1976.

Ruether, Rosemary R. *Woman Guides: Readings toward a Feminist Theology*. Boston: Beacon Press, 1985.

Russell, Letty M. *The Future of Partnership*. Philadelphia: Westminster Press, 1979.

———. *The Liberating Word: A Guide to Non-Sexist Interpretation of the Bible*. Philadelphia: Westminster Press, 1976.

CASE
4

IS POLYGAMY
MORAL?

There I sat, gasping for air in a small green station wagon crowded with people as the vehicle sped dangerously along a dark and winding road in a rural community about ten miles northeast of Nairobi. It was getting a bit late, about eight o'clock in the evening. Pulling up to my destination, I hurriedly got out and briskly walked up to a gray, frame and brick building, well-lighted and maintained. It was the community center where I was to meet three women who had agreed to talk with me informally about the sensitive issue of polygamy in African culture. I came up the steps, rang the doorbell several times, and waited. Soon a security guard appeared.

"Excuse me, sir. Is this the community center?" I inquired.

"Yes," he answered as he opened the door widely. "Come right in; we've been expecting you."

I was escorted to a well-lighted, modestly decorated conference room furnished with antique English chairs and Victorian leather sofas. Lovely paintings and batiks depicting patterns of life and culture in traditional African society hung on the walls. Soon the three women I was to meet entered the conference room. At first, we were rather nervous but composed and soon began to get acquainted with one another over tea and cookies. They all spoke superb English, though their indigenous language was Swahili. The women were not strangers to each other but had grown up in communities not far apart in the central province of Kenya. Polite yet intellectually assertive, these African women, I discovered, have conflicting beliefs and deep feelings about the issue of polygamy, and its role and function in African culture and family life.

The question, Is polygamy moral? is asked in an attempt to better understand and grapple with this age-old dilemma, from an ethical perspective and in dialogue. Now after we had exchanged greetings, our conversation became serious.

A brief word about the background of each woman seems appropriate. Ruth Muthoni is a thirty-four-year-old mother of five, married to Robert Muthoni, a banker. On the surface they appear to have a stable relationship and a good marriage. Her husband, Robert, owns property in the rural village community where she lives and cares for the family. Because of the demands and pressures of his job, Robert stays in the city of Nairobi most of the time. While Ruth suspects that other women are in Robert's life, she dismisses the issue, saying, "Men will be men . . . and I don't try and keep tabs on him every day or night."

Margaret Wanjiku is a twenty-eight-year-old divorcee and mother of two, who grew up in a Christian home. Although she feels that her parents were not overly protective on matters of sex and morals, they were, nevertheless, strict. Her father is dead now, but he was a faithful elder in their local Presbyterian church and a respected schoolteacher in the community. Margaret's mother was a devoted housewife.

Helen Wambui, the third woman in the group, is a twenty-one-year-old college student in her second year of study in accounting. Aggressive and full of life, her career goals include traveling abroad, working for a big business firm in the area of management, and owning a house and a car. Helen is the mother of one child out of wedlock. About her child, Helen feels confident about the future: "I don't see my child as a big burden or social stigma. It was something that just happened."

What follows is a group dialogue in response to the question, What do you think or feel about polygamy today?

RUTH: I really don't see what the big fuss is over polygamy; as long as I can remember it has always been around, and not just in Africa. Somewhere I read or was told that the system of polygamy was practiced in virtually all cultures at one time or another. Besides, it was even practiced in ancient biblical times, I believe. So, I don't see anything necessarily wrong with it even now.

MARGARET: Come on, Ruth, how can you be so simple-minded, old-fashioned, and carefree about the seriousness of the issue these days. The morality of polygamy is a big problem for all of us.

RUTH: But, I am serious.

MARGARET: OK, but your views on the issue leave me with an uneasy conscience; all of the talk about polygamy being so common among different societies doesn't really appeal to me. And I'm not that sure about how accurate your information is when you generalize by saying that "virtually all societies have practiced it." The fact of the matter is I really can't see how any person, especially women in these modern times, can go for such a thing. After all, because of the way things are today, polygamy seems to be a slowly dying thing in modern African societies.

RUTH: I grant you that we are living in modern times and that the world has changed a great deal . . . but you still ignore the fact that polygamy is the traditional African way of family life. Remember, it was a vital part of our moral values, especially in helping to provide guidance for our boys and girls about their roles in community life. Plus, it was a way of sharing and giving responsibility among the wives for the common good in our various kinship groups [hbari]. Further, I feel that in our traditional culture the children didn't have the sort of problems that they have today in modern society—and in the urban parts of our country. Now I see problems of drinking, drugs, crime, child abuse, and all sorts of things that our children didn't have to be bothered with then. I feel that the reason is that polygamy actually helped to keep a lot of kids out of trouble because it operated as an "extended family." You know, Margaret, polygamy has always been, to some extent, a sign of wealth and blessing in our traditional culture and religion.

In the heat of the group discussion on the morality of polygamy, Helen was beginning to feel frustrated and uneasy. Shifting her body from side to side, she wondered how Ruth and Margaret could be at such extremes. Until now, she had not been able to say anything. "Wait a minute friends, you both are just going at each other, and it's confusing," she interrupted.

HELEN: I am not sure if we have gotten under the surface of this hard issue. All I hear so far is a bundle of words, a sort of cat and mouse game back and forth. Well, there are many ways of looking at polygamy; each one suits someone's fancy. I think that the man, the husband, has the advantage, regardless of how you look at it. Literally, the idea itself means that the husband has the privilege of more than one wife at the same time. It doesn't make good sense in my book to be giving all of that advantage to the man! Naturally, *they* see it a different way. After all, it was the men folks who set up this social arrangement for control over family life; it seems that we have always been in abundant supply for our men folks, in traditional African society . . . Even as you grow up as a child and begin to have fun with the opposite sex, there never seems to be enough boys to go around—whether they treat you nice or not. So then, this custom of plural marriages fits well into the male way of doing things and their control over us.

RUTH: That view of the custom of polygamy may be fine for you, but I don't see it that way.

MARGARET: Neither do I, altogether. In our modern times, I can't see how polygamy is an advantage to anybody! It is a slowly passing lifestyle that few African men can really afford.

HELEN: Granted there are tensions in our churches and the wider society on this issue, but I feel that everyone must be free to choose—to each his own; maybe a refreshing view would be to avoid being a slave to either polygamy or monogamy. After all, aren't there some societies that give the advantage to the woman? A chance for her to have as many husbands as she wants? Maybe, that's really something I could go for . . . It may be less troublesome.

MARGARET: But that's not our issue here tonight.

RUTH: Nevertheless, Helen's point is well taken; and some of the feelings she expressed I agree with. But I don't agree that polygamy serves useful purposes for men or husbands only. There is more to it than that. I don't think you understand me that well; I've been trying to say that polygamy is okay because it helps our children to develop, to learn something about sharing, about responsibility and how to get along with others in the community. Indeed, I feel that children from polygamous households fare much better socially than those from monogamous households. So you see, in the old days, it was really more than the question of social advantage for the male. Polygamy, then, really had significance for the whole community; it kept together the bonds of kinship. That makes polygamy a natural thing for both African men and women and is in no way immoral.

MARGARET: I have been pondering what you and Helen have been saying, and I am troubled that there is such a big difference in your views. In the first place, Ruth, I really can't see, for the life of me, how you can say that polygamy is so "natural"; even in the old days of colonialism some of our people questioned then how natural it was. Natural for whom? . . . I still don't think that it is right when our public leaders in church and society tell us to move all the way toward modern development and have us believe that this will somehow solve our problem of polygamy . . . Besides, I find polygamy so unchristian.

HELEN: Well, you may be stretching the point a bit to say that it is "unchristian." What's so unchristian about polygamy? Many of the ancient biblical stories I have read seem to condone the marital practice. Didn't certain men of God engage in the practice according to the Old Testament? I seem to remember something about that?

MARGARET: Yes, I think that it was condoned in biblical times out of necessity. But that was, you see, the old law of Moses; we now live under the new law of Christ. Under the old law of the Hebrews there were many things tolerated, but not necessarily right or honorable.

RUTH: Honorable? I don't understand why you would say that polygamy is not honorable, Margaret; you seem to have lost your African roots altogether! Our traditional elders gone-on would roll over in their graves, if someone would dare say that having more than one wife was dishonorable!

MARGARET: You misunderstood me; I didn't mean it that way.

RUTH: So, what did you really mean?

MARGARET: I mean when our sisters today are itching, because of many problems, nobody needs to tell them where to scratch! I mean just because polygamy was tolerated in ancient biblical times, for different reasons, doesn't mean that it is the ideal thing for African Christians today. What I know about the New Testament from my own minister is that Christ expects more from us today . . . Christ calls us to a higher moral way for the family and all of marriage. I remember my minister quoting the gospel of Matthew as saying: "You have heard that it was said, you shall not commit adultery, but I say to you that everyone who looks at a woman lustfully has already committed adultery with her in his heart." (See Matt. 5:27.)

RUTH: Come now, Margaret, how can you call polygamy adultery and against God's will when it was practiced by many of the fathers of the faith? Jacob and many other Bible characters seemed to have gone along with the practice. (See Gen. 3:1–21.) So I don't see anything wrong with it in African society today, if a man can afford it . . . After all, did not the Bible say that all things should be shared in common?

HELEN: I'm not sure, because sometimes when you try and be too good and share all things in common, people end up getting hurt. Besides, such an ideal is not realistic and creates more tensions among the wives.

MARGARET: But that's beside the point, Helen. I still feel that the practice of polygamy is sinful, and the ones who enter into it are committing adultery. (See Exod. 20:14; Deut. 5:18.)

HELEN: Margaret, I really don't think it's right the way you are using the Bible and quoting scripture and all—just to prove your point. The Bible can't be reduced to some old-fashioned rule book, can it?

MARGARET: Well, that may be easy for you to say but I still feel that the practice is unchristian; for example, what if a husband is unfair and shows favor to one wife and neglects another? What if a husband no longer wants wife B and her children; would he just exclude wife B and throw her and the children into the streets to fend for themselves? Both you and I know that those things sometimes happen in polygamous households.

RUTH: I never thought about it quite that way; yet I still have problems with your views that polygamy is unchristian . . . If that were the case, there would be far fewer Christians in African churches today! The churches I know about would be excluding, then, a big portion of their membership!

MARGARET: Well, I can't respond to that at all; it is just the way I feel about it as a Christian myself.

HELEN: I don't agree or feel that way. The whole system of plural marriages is a man's pleasure game. It entirely ignores the needs of children in our global community, as more people find themselves moving about—from the rural areas to city life. This creates so much confusion and insecurity for everybody, especially our children.

MARGARET: Yes, you do have a good point.

RUTH: But that still doesn't resolve the question, Is polygamy moral?

MARGARET: I still agonize greatly over the question of polygamy. You wonder just which way is the best.

RUTH: Well, I don't see that much wrong with it, as far as I can see; you know all the folks in traditional African society took real pride in the budding of new seeds into the family. There is an old African proverb which says, "God gave women wonderful seeds of life, the more the seeds, the better the life!"

MARGARET: Well, there is also an old Christian adage I once heard an elder of my village say regarding marriage: It is better to suffer under one wife than to have the envy of many!

HELEN: Well, sisters, it's getting rather late in the evening, and I don't think we can solve this issue tonight, at least to everyone's satisfaction.

DISCUSSION NOTES

The regular discussion leader may observe that one of the pivotal issues in this dialogical case is the *right* of African women to self-determination and moral choice. For African women, like their male counterparts, the idea of moral choice is not perceived as individual but as communal in character. In African culture, moral choice for women is rooted in the larger social fabric and involves respect for family values, village customs, the authority of elders, and the deep impact of traditional religion upon all aspects of life and work.

As the case would suggest, the reader may want to pay particular attention to the shifting paradigm, mood, and changing attitudes toward the traditional pattern of polygamy in African life and society. I think that logic legitimates the claim that the viability and function of polygamy for both women and men in contemporary African society is largely influenced by the economic factor. It seems to me that in traditional African society, the moral question was never, What is the value or worth of polygamy? because polygamy as a form of family life and identity had virtue and practical value in and of itself. Rather, the difficult moral question for contemporary African women is simply, What is the *price* of polygamy today in a society experiencing unparalleled internal political, social, and economic change?

Meaningful group discussion could focus on the emerging roles, perceptions, and identity of women in contemporary African society today. Crucial to our own struggle and reflection is the ethical issue of education. Should African women and men have equal access to the benefits of education? For doing ethics and theology in the global community, the question is both intriguing and provocative because it raises once again the perennial themes and concerns of faith and liberation. Gradually but persistently, today's African women are overcoming the historic lack of equal access to education.

I conclude this "teaching note" with a relevant point made by Dr. Christiana I. Parker, who has done research on the progress of contemporary African women:

> Historically, the West African woman (as all other Black African women) has been portrayed in western societies as being uneducated, barefoot, stoop-shouldered and somewhat fat. In fact, if liberation for women worldwide means the freedom to work, rather than from work, she is then the most liberated woman in the world.[1]

NOTES

1. In Joan Matthews, "West African Women Need to Overcome Historic Lack of Education," *Black Issues in Higher Education* 5 (September 1988), 12.

Ethical Approach

1. Which approach would you likely use in addressing the issue of polygamy?
2. As a Christian or student of the Bible, is one approach just as good as another?
3. As a counselor or pastor, what biblical method in particular seems appropriate for the increase of global awareness?

Issues for Reflection

1. How would you clarify the issues at stake between Ruth, Margaret, and Helen?
2. On what grounds would you say polygamy is moral or immoral?
3. Would you have concerns regarding children from polygamous households? If so, what would they be?

SUGGESTED READING

Angelou, Maya. *And Still I Rise*. New York: Random House, 1978.

Davis, Angela. *Women, Race, and Class*. New York: Vintage Books, 1981.

Eichelberger, William L. "Voice of Black Feminism." *Quest: A Feminist Quarterly* 3 (Spring 1977).

Feldman, Harold, and Margaret Feldman, eds. *Current Controversies in Marriage and Family*. Beverly Hills, Calif.: Sage Publications, 1985.

Giddings, Paula. *When and Where I Enter*. New York: William Morrow, 1984.

Grant, Jacquelyn. "Black Theology and the Black Woman." In *Black Theology: A Documentary History, 1966–1979*, edited by Gayraud S. Wilmore and James H. Cone. Maryknoll, N.Y.: Orbis Books, 1979.

Harley, Sharon, and R. Terborg-Penn, eds. *Afro-American Women*. New York: Kennikat Press, 1978.

Hillman, Eugene. *Pastoral Perspectives in Eastern Africa after Vatican II*. Nairobi, Kenya: Amecea, 1967.

———. *Polygamy Reconsidered*. Maryknoll, N.Y.: Orbis Books, 1975.

Wallace, Michelle. *Black Macho and the Myth of the Superwoman*. New York: Dial Press, 1978.

Wimberly, Edward P. "Pastoral Counseling and the Black Perspective." In *African American Religious Studies: An Interdisciplinary Anthology*, edited by Gayraud S. Wilmore. Durham, N.C.: Duke University Press, 1989.

CASE

5

SECOND
LOVE

It was easy to empathize with Ann Warjini, a twenty-nine-year-old
housewife, who stormed into the pastor's study just steps in front of her
husband, complaining that she had had enough of his unfaithfulness!
Sam, her husband, had been having an affair with Freda Sobiti, an
attractive brown-skinned woman, twenty-five years of age. Ann's voice
was filled with rage as she poured out her heart to Pastor Okello, senior
minister of the Oakridge Presbyterian Church, Nairobi, Kenya. Without
even waiting to be asked to sit, Ann announced loudly to her pastor,
"You can't imagine the nightmare I've been going through the last six
months with Sam; he has literally been impossible to live with since I
found out about his outside lover—and this time, I'm not going to forgive
him no matter how many times he crawls back and tells his syrupy lies!"

The Warjinis, regular members of the church for the past ten months,
moved to Nairobi two years before from the coastal area of Kenya. They
live in a sprawling middle-class neighborhood that is bursting with new
housing and suburban shopping centers. They came to Nairobi for the job
opportunities in their professions. Their occupational and social profiles
would suggest that this young couple would be emotionally and psycho-
logically compatible. They seem to be blessed with no more vices or
virtues than any average middle-class couple. Both Sam and Ann are
from well-to-do families, a far cry from the nameless mass of humanity
that daily roams Nairobi's streets, begging for a few shillings to buy bread
or an ear of roasted corn. Oh, no! Quite to the contrary, Sam and Ann
are from a social stratum in Kenyan society that can likely afford a maid,
a gardener, a security guard, and an errand boy. In the post-independence
period that emerged on the heels of the demise of colonialism, European

imperialism, and the gradual passing of the old order, Kenya produced its own ruling elite. Now, Sam and Ann are not, by any stretch of the imagination, a part of that "ruling elite," but they are ambitious climbers of the social ladder.

Sam Warjini is a banker, and his wife, Ann, is an elementary education teacher. She is currently a housewife, between jobs, and hopes to enter the workforce later. Outwardly, they appear to have all the marks of success and a happy marriage. They have a degree of social respectability in their community. Their two daughters, Nykol, 8, and Monika, 6, attend private school.

However, a closer look at the life of the Warjini family indicated, as Pastor Okello suspected, a couple in distress and near the breaking point. Despite the outer signs of financial security and the veneer of social respectability, Ann was feeling emptiness and numbness because of her husband's infidelity. She lamented to Pastor Okello, "When Sam and I got married eight years ago, we were so happy and full of energy; we did things together and shared our hopes and dreams. And though I was six-months pregnant with our first born, Nykol, that didn't seem to bother Sam. Instead that was all the more reason to get married—at least I felt that way at the time."

Meanwhile, Sam just sat on the sofa in silence, a look of disgust mingled with shame on his face. In fact, for some reason, Sam uttered hardly a word throughout the first counseling session. Pastor Okello probed further, asking Ann, "What happened next?"

Ann briskly replied, "Well, I inadvertently discovered through a close friend of mine that my husband, even in the late stages of my first pregnancy, was having an affair with Freda. Maybe I was stupid at the time, but I really didn't let on that I knew because I didn't want to spoil things for us, especially since the baby was coming."

Tears poured from Ann's eyes. "I really was not facing reality at the time; I was just fooling myself into believing that Sam would let go of the affair with Freda . . . He promised me that things would get better . . . Today I'm fed up because neither has come true!" Ann's voice was near a whisper. "Maybe I still love Sam, but my feelings are so mixed up."

By now, fifteen minutes of the session had gone by, and Sam still sat on the sofa staring aimlessly out the window. Suddenly, he broke his silence. "What use is it for me to speak, since Ann just blurted out all of our personal problems!" Throughout Ann's narrative, Pastor Okello had observed Sam's emotional state. He was visibly disturbed about the problem and was apparently agonizing over what action he should take.

Sam's sentiments were evident, though he desperately tried to cover them.

In a subsequent private counseling session, to the surprise and shock of Pastor Okello, Sam disclosed that Freda Sobiti, his "second love," was three months pregnant. Obviously, one can imagine that in the eyes of his minister this only added insult to injury. Sam reluctantly admitted the gravity of his misdeeds and confessed that he wished to amend his ways. In the presence of God and Pastor Okello, Sam promised to do better for his wife.

Concerned about the chances for reconciliation and aware of the Warjini's steadily deteriorating marriage, Pastor Okello promised Sam that he would not mention Freda's pregnancy to Ann, especially since neither Freda nor Sam had decided what action to take. From Pastor Okello's point of view, the only thing that Sam appeared to be fairly certain about was his desire to save his crumbling marriage.

As counselor and pastor in this situation, Pastor Okello felt a bit uneasy, primarily because Sam had made similar promises and moral declarations before, which had amounted to very little. As a pastor of Oakridge Presbyterian Church for several years, he had learned that generally a married man looks different when he is with his mistress. So Pastor Okello was not without doubts regarding Sam's promises and good intentions. Yet in a gesture of good faith, he arranged another counseling session with the couple in a last attempt at reconciliation. Appearing uneasy, they both agreed to come to his office again for conversation and counseling.

This time, Sam and Ann sat at opposite ends of the sofa, facing Pastor Okello. Ann seemed to have made some progress—if ever so slight—since the first session; at least she was outwardly poised. "Go ahead, Reverend, you called us here together," she said.

"I feel that it is important for the two of you to talk over your differences, especially for the sake of the children. They love you both," advised Pastor Okello. "Besides, I would hate to see more frustration and hurt grow between you. Didn't Christ admonish all of us as Christians to practice forgiveness and kindness? Are we not required to try and work our problems out in the spirit of Christian love?" Ann glanced at Sam but said nothing. Both appeared to be trying to figure out who should make the next move, walking into the dark of the night not knowing where the next step would lead. Pastor Okello reasoned inwardly that if they were going to have a good Christian marriage—if a marriage at all— real movement toward honest and open communication must take place.

Before ending the session, Pastor Okello reminded them, in the idiomatic Swahili expression: "Wagombanao ndio wapatanao" (Those who quarrel are those who make up).

[NOTE: In light of the communal emphasis in the African religio-cultural tradition, Edward P. Wimberly, in *Pastoral Care in the Black Church*, describes four important functions of pastoral care in a given counseling situation. These four functions consist of *healing, sustaining, guiding*, and *reconciliation*. The reader must be attentive to these interrelated functions of care in the attempt to restore a condition of health and wholeness to relationships which have been injured emotionally, morally, or spiritually. There is in this case, as well as in others, a need to identify certain useful steps in the counseling process. A suggested order may include:

1. The person or couple enters counseling.
2. The couple needs communal support and direction. (In the African religio-cultural tradition, pastoral care is a communal concept and activity; it does not take place in clinical isolation but rather it exists whenever persons minister to one another in need or at a point of crisis.)
3. Open communication: Sam and Ann need to work at genuine dialogue in order to reestablish basic trust in the marriage.
4. The couple needs space in the relationship to identify and sort out the critical issues.
5. Movement toward reconciliation: the desire to move from hurt to healing must be a mutual endeavor on the part of the person or couple involved.]

DISCUSSION NOTES

Throughout this book I have emphasized some of the significant parallels and tensions between indigenous African family values and the black community in America. Many African values and social patterns tend to influence and shape the way men and women relate to each other in the African-American community. To the African identity and role differentiation are the result of a person's interaction with nature and the environment. The traditional African community plays a crucial role in establishing the moral and social boundaries of male-female relationships and marital fidelity or infidelity. Noted African scholar John Mbiti has pointed out that certain rituals and ceremonies are the main instruments by which male-female boundaries are established for the good of the marriage and the stability of community. Hence, the pastoral counseling question of love and fidelity is also a *communal question* as well.

All actions, both the morally "out of bounds" and those that are morally permissible, deeply affect not just a particular marriage, here, Sam and Ann Warjini's, but also the fabric of community life. Thus, I must point out that during regular group discussion of this case on the problems and hurts of infidelity, Sam and Ann's problems must not be seen purely from the personal perspective of specific counseling models of the West. Like the ceremonial naming of a child, the experience of marriage or the test of marriage as symbolized in this case is a community event in African society. In this case, there are also important counseling issues pertaining to the loss of marital trust and esteem, anger and hurt, and the uneasy promise of reconciliation.

Reading this as a case in pastoral counseling, one may want to be especially attentive to its social-ethical dimension. Regardless of one's particular approach to this case, I want to point out that the four traditional forms of pastoral care—healing, guiding, sustaining, and reconciling—must be performed within the wider religio-cultural context of African life. Thus, the idea of genuine pastoral care for a hurting African couple must always be rooted in a caring community. In this sense, no one is ever cut off from the mediating and sustaining values of the community.

An especially helpful resource to use in discussing this case is Edward Wimberly's book, *Pastoral Counseling and Spiritual Values: A Black Point of View*.

Ethical Approach

1. As a Christian counselor, how would you handle Ann's anger and deep hurt?
2. What must Sam do to solve the unrevealed problem of Freda's pregnancy?

Issues for Reflection

1. What are the real issues and dilemmas in this case?
2. Did Pastor Okello err in his counseling?
3. When should confidentiality be broken?

SUGGESTED READING

Bok, Sissela. *Lying*. New York: Random House, 1978.

Browning, Don S. *The Moral Context of Pastoral Care*. Philadelphia: Westminster Press, 1976.

———. *Religious Ethics and Pastoral Care*. Philadelphia: Westminster Press, 1983.

Carroll, Jackson W. *Ministry as Reflective Practice*. Washington, D.C.: The Alban Institute, 1986.

Dittes, James E. *Minister on the Spot*. Philadelphia: Pilgrim Press, 1970.

Firet, Jacob. *Dynamics in Pastoring*. Grand Rapids: Wm. B. Eerdmans, 1986.

Goldman, Alan H. *The Moral Foundations of Professional Ethics*. Totowa, N.J.: Rowan & Littlefield, 1980.

Noyce, Gaylord. *Pastoral Ethics*. Nashville: Abingdon Press, 1988.

Oates, Wayne. *The Christian Pastor*. Philadelphia: Westminster Press, 1963.

Wimberly, Edward P. *Pastoral Care in the Black Church*. Nashville: Abingdon Press, 1979.

———. *Pastoral Counseling and Spiritual Values: A Black Point of View*. Nashville: Abingdon Press, 1982.

CASE

6

UNKNOWN PATHWAYS
IN SEARCH OF EDUCATION

In the dark of the night, Paul Ruot Kor, a tall, slender man with dark, fine features and muscular shoulders, sat on a bench in the airport in the southern province of the Sudan nervously waiting for his plane to arrive. Paul was not alone in the almost empty airport; there were seven other modestly dressed young men, who ranged in age from twenty-three to thirty-one, in Paul's party. These young African men shared one goal: to fly from Nasir to the Malaikal province in order to take a qualifying exam for entrance into St. Paul's Theological College. For reasons they never discovered, the plane did not arrive. The men estimated the traveling distance between Nasir and Malakal to be approximately 225 miles; perhaps the actual distance was more—Paul was not sure. However, there was one thing that this party of eight was sure of and in agreement on: they had to be at a designated place at a certain time if their dream of a theological education was to become a reality! According to Paul, to whom I spoke, it was imperative that the party of eight make the journey to Malakal.

Now, in the dark of night, the only option for the eight men was to walk, by toil and sweat and the pain of aching feet, the 225 miles from Nasir to Malakal. After each man had followed the ritual of taking counsel with the other, the first steps of the long, tedious journey began. On that night in the early spring of 1985, Paul emerged as the group's leader. They nervously embarked upon an uncharted journey which was to last five days and five nights—without rest and with very little water or food. Paul and his friends struggled and clawed out unknown pathways through the forest and across riverbeds, over rough terrain that could only be described as "tempestuously dangerous!"

The goal shared by the men—as they mounted steep ridges and endured dust storms peppered with rain—was the rare opportunity for theological education in service to God and suffering humanity. Despite sleepless nights and constant danger, Paul and his friends completed the journey. It was not without its trying moments, however. For example, Paul and his companions walked three days without any water. In some places along the way, there were robbers on the road who shot and killed innocent village people, but none of the eight people who made the journey was injured or harmed. Paul regarded this as a miracle and saw the mighty hand of God at work in his life. The men took the qualifying exam and a few weeks later returned to St. Paul's Theological College. For better or worse, their dream of acquiring a theological education had already begun.

While this is a story of the uncommon courage and determination of eight men from the Sudan, the major focus of this case study is the faith pilgrimage and struggles of Paul Ruot Kor. Paul, who has made a sound profession of faith, had a difficult childhood, and as we have seen, his road to seminary was not easy.

Paul is thirty-four years old. He is happily married to Sarah Nyowuor Kuon, who is twenty-three; they are the loving parents of two children, Tabilha, 3, and Henry, 2. Paul was born and reared in the community of Nasir on the River Sobat. Nasir has a population of approximately 20,000 people. Nomadic by circumstance and cultural conditions, many of the people of Nasir are relegated to lives of poverty, disease, and social deprivation as a result of environmental factors, religious conflicts, and political realities that baffle this troubled nation-state. Paul's immediate family is from the Nuer tribe. Paul's family includes his mother, Martha Nyagony Kuac, and his father, Kor Won. In addition, the family was blessed with six daughters who bear the family name—Rebeca Nyajuaoni Kor, Mary Nyabuol Kor, Sarah Nyakong Kor, Nyachuol Kor, and Elizabeth Nyalam Kor.

As a child (and the eldest), Paul experienced the pain of poverty and social deprivation as he struggled, along with other members of his family, to survive. "Education was virtually nonexistent and those few that got it did not get much," he said. Thus the best a young person could do was to work the land. Indeed, most of the people in Paul's village community did just that: they worked hard on the *mun* (land). The staples that affluent Western nations take for granted—adequate food and water, clothes, shelter, and medical services—were either in short supply or nonexistent.

Paul was taught by his mother, Martha Nyagony Kuac, that, in order to survive, people of the "river valley" must learn how to swim with the current. His mother would caution him with a traditional saying: "Remember Paul, water cannot climb a hill, it can only flow downward into the valley." From his perspective as an adult, Paul realizes that what he came to terms with as a young lad of ten was what every human being, if lucky, confronts, namely, the burden of and need for self-knowledge and the will to do whatever is necessary to survive. For Paul, childhood was no "crystal stair." He described himself as a "ten-year-old lad, going on twenty-one!" Even as a child he had to be a man—quickly!

Obviously, for a young boy in the village community of Nasir, the social environment was a vulnerable one. According to his testimony, Paul coped with the death-dealing elements of the environment through prayer and faith in God. Like many of his contemporaries, Paul had an uneven and difficult childhood. As a young and innocent boy, Paul had an experience that deeply influenced his social development and had a powerful impact on his moral character: When he was ten, John Chuol, an evangelist, became Paul's teacher, and influenced him in a positive way.

With the constant reminders of death and poverty all around, young Paul became deeply concerned about the doctrine of the resurrection. In the religion of his Nuer childhood, there was no doctrine of life after death or anything similar to it. Ironically, Paul came to a personal knowledge of Jesus Christ as Lord and Liberator amidst the failures and contradictions of life. Because of his constant groping with his fears of death, the faith question for young Paul was not theoretical or academic. The concreteness of faith seemed to function as a sustaining power as Paul confronted the daily realities of poverty and disease. However, unholy misery and intimidation were still constant companions on the pathways he walked as a child. (Some writers and scholars, such as John Mbiti and Ali Mazrui, remind us that in the African worldview there is no radical separation between the "physical and metaphysical" images of reality. For the most part, these writers—to our amazement or despair—tend to avoid the Cartesian dualism so common in the philosophical and theological traditions of the West.)

"Before I met John Chuol, no one told me that there was life after death," says Paul with a look of astonishment on his face, as if he were reliving the experience. Through the evangelistic work of the Rev. Chuol, Paul learned how to read. "It was a tremendous joy!" Paul recalls. At this point in our conversation, Paul broke into a warm smile, leaned forward in his seat, and said, "I can't count the times I thanked God for Reverend Chuol and his ministry in my life, and how he almost single-handedly brought me to Christ." Paul went on to confess, "Jesus is the Lord of my life . . . and all I try to do is trust his promises, especially when I'm having a difficult problem of some kind. Here, I always go back to Reverend Chuol's words of how I can put my trust in God. He would say, 'With God, you lack nothing!' " Now, as an adult reflecting on these childhood experiences, Paul Ruot Kor believes that his encounter with John Chuol made the difference in his young life and provided a basis of assurance and security in a childhood world filled with so much insecurity, pain, and death. According to Paul, the scripture that was key to his self-understanding as a minister and that guided his faith journey was the Gospel of John. John 11:25–27 was particularly instructive for his faith and life:

> Jesus said to her, "I am the resurrection and the life; he who believes in me, though he die, yet shall he live, and whoever lives and believes in me shall never die. Do you believe this?" She said to him, "yes, Lord; I believe that you are the Christ, the son of God."

In 1977, Paul Ruot Kor was authorized by the Presbyterian church of his village community to be a volunteer evangelist in the work of ministry, especially with young adults. Paul sees his ministry as one of social outreach, touching the lives of people and meeting their needs. As a seminarian and now as a minister, his main concern in ministry has been to develop a way by which people in his village community back home can keep alive their traditional stories and customs. For Paul, this is a source of both challenge and pain, because so much of the old tradition is being lost or neglected in Africa's uncritical embrace of Western technology and social values. He recognizes the value of technology but sees it wreaking havoc on traditional African values. He worries about century-old traditions as he raises the question, Will there be anything worth passing on to future generations?

I observed that Paul also appeared to be alarmed about an uncritical fundamentalism among his fellow seminarians on the campus in the 1980s. He lamented, "Upon my arrival on campus, I felt like I was being pulled into certain camps of thought. I don't see myself as a fundamentalist, but an evangelist in service of God and the needy." He seemed further disturbed when he confessed, "I feel that too much fundamentalism can drive good people away from the church—and get them all confused about their own customs and traditions. At least I feel uneasy about that.

What am I to do? I feel real pressure to make a choice between my tradition back home and the fundamentalist Christianity among some students here . . . In my view it takes a bold man to renounce his own tradition."

DISCUSSION NOTES

While the background for our reflections is the story of eight African Christians in search of education, the case centers on the life and faith pilgrimage of Paul Ruot Kor, a Sudanese student at St. Paul's United Theological College in Limuru, Kenya. It seems more important, at times, to offer people the opportunity to share moments of personal faith and challenge than to focus exclusively on the goal of achieving formal education. The story of Paul Ruot Kor involves dimensions of both head and heart.

In one sense, this case is a lesson in the deeper meaning of education—learning done not so much in the secure environment of a structured classroom but along the journey and amidst the danger of life lived at the edge. It is not a case study about faith as a *tool of reason*, but one on reason as a tool of faith as demonstrated in the protracted struggle by eight men to survive and to reach their destination.

Some of the overarching issues that may enhance regular case discussion include:

1. The spirit of self-determination demonstrated by eight Sudanese students as they waited nervously in an airport for a plane that never arrived.

2. The grave uncertainty the men felt when faced with the sudden necessity of journeying more than two hundred miles—step by step—from Nasir to Malakal.

3. The unwelcome test of faith and courage as the "party of eight" was forced by circumstances to become a "nomadic community," fashioned together by their struggle to survive a difficult terrain.

4. The shaping influence of John Chuol, the evangelist, in the formative years of young Paul Ruot Kor.

5. The haunting thought of death in Paul's life and faith as he attempted to make sense of the doctrine of resurrection.

6. Paul's theological probing as a seminarian to come to terms with the problems of fundamentalism and Christianity, on one hand, and the confusion and concern about African customs and traditions, on the other.

To be sure, these are only a few of the issues that demand attention in the discussion of this case. But they can provide individuals with a point of departure for serious dialogue and the sharing of personal faith.

In further study on issues of faith and liberation, some people may find helpful Joseph Healey's book, *A Fifth Gospel: The Experience of Black Christian Values* (Maryknoll, N.Y.: Orbis Books, 1981).

Ethical Approach

1. What ethical concerns do you find pertinent in this case?
2. What approach to the Bible would you find useful given the problems of fundamentalism in church and society today?
3. Is Paul's concern about fundamentalism justified?

Issues for Reflection

1. What connections do you see between church evangelism and the needs of the poor in developing countries?
2. Sketch out a plan for understanding the value and burden of your own tradition.
3. In your view, what is the relationship between Christianity and traditional African culture? What should it be?

SUGGESTED READING

Dorson, Richard. *African Folklore*. New York: Doubleday & Co., 1972.

DuBois, W.E.B. *The World and Africa: An Inquiry into the Part Which Africa Has Played in World History*. New York: Kraus International, 1976.

Dundes, Alan. *The Study of Folklore*. Englewood Cliffs, N.J.: Prentice-Hall, 1965.

Evans, Alice F., Robert A. Evans, and William B. Kennedy. *Pedagogies for the Non-Poor*. Maryknoll, N.Y.: Orbis Books, 1987.

Lord, Albert. *The Singer of Tales*. New York: Atheneum, 1973.

Mbiti, John S. *An Introduction to African Religion*. London and Portsmouth, N.H.: Heinemann Educational Books, 1975.

Ngugi, wa Thiong'o. *Devil on the Cross*. London: Heinemann Educational Books, 1982.

Shannon, David T., and Gayraud S. Wilmore, eds. *Black Witness to Apostolic Faith*. Grand Rapids: Wm. B. Eerdmans, 1985.

Umeasiegbu, Rems N. *The Way We Lived*. London: Heinemann Educational Books, 1969.

———. *Words Are Sweet*. Nairobi, Kenya: East African Publishing House, 1980.

CASE
7

A STRANGER
AT WORSHIP

"I guess I'll get up early and go to morning worship and communion at St. Andrew's Episcopal Church," I thought. It was the first time I had been to this service, for I had recently been sent as an American missionary to Nairobi, Kenya, East Africa. I knew no one; and no one knew who I, John Lawson, was, either.

The worship service began promptly at nine o'clock with a familiar congregational hymn. The senior pastor and his lay assistants emerged from the back of the sanctuary joyfully chanting "Holy, Holy, Holy." They were formally robed in purple and white with an assortment of regalia matched for the occasion. Pastor Kwasi Imbundi led the procession with grace and splendor. Pastor Imbundi's eyes seemed to scrutinize everyone as he passed down the aisle among the people, walking gently with a hymn book in his right hand and a gold-laced cross in his left hand. The sanctuary was bone-chilling cold; people huddled together in the pews to keep warm and to ward off the early morning dampness. Many wore sweaters, scarves, and coats, for the church was without heat. The sanctuary was sparsely populated, and I ended up sitting in a pew alone, near the center aisle. Pastor Imbundi mounted the pulpit as the congregation sang the last verse of the hymn, "Holy, Holy, Holy"; his back was perfectly arched. "Well, so far so good," I reflected.

Then, suddenly, I realized that I had made a mistake. I had come to the Swahili service, thinking that it was the English. I learned only later that the English service was at 11:00 o'clock each Sunday morning and that St. Andrew's begins each worship service with a hymn in English as a multilingual teaching tool for youth and adults. I glanced hurriedly at the order of worship in the bulletin as we were about to recite "prayers of confession," which would be followed by "scripture reading" and the second congregational hymn. That hymn was to be performed in Swahili.

As a newcomer, I knew only one word in Swahili—*jambo*, or "hello." A certain uneasiness gripped me for there was no one else in my pew to help shield or cover up my awkwardness as I tried to utter words of praise and adoration to God in a strange tongue! I sat nervously on the edge of a lonely pew, my face frozen, desperately trying to echo the words of the songs coming from the lips of Pastor Imbundi, a man tall and slender, with a strong, melodic voice. Embarrassed, I thought, "No, no . . . I don't believe this, I've jumped into something over my head. I don't know what to do." My thoughts came quickly. "Should I attempt to leave the service quietly and run the risk of offending the worshiping community? Or should I stay and pretend all is well? Is it possible to worship God without understanding the words I offer up in praise?" The questions kept coming. "Is it an affront to my own integrity to stay? Am I murmuring phrases and chants as a fake? Should I rush out of the sanctuary and take a crash course in Swahili? Why do I feel angry and embarrassed?"

In the chill of the morning, I felt really alone, a sort of pilgrim stranger amidst the people of St. Andrew's. As we prayed, sang hymns, and made our confessions before the presence of a loving and merciful God, I felt cut off by the gap between American and African culture. I did not feel a cozy alliance because the liturgy was set in a social context alien to me. Then, as Pastor Imbundi took his text and began his sermon, I remembered what one of my homiletics professors had said to me long ago: "Christian worship is not so much a matter of comprehending the mystery of God as it is praising and serving God in life. . . Worship is a time of paying attention to the acts of God." I was elated by the thought of worship as attentiveness of head and heart to God's activity, although I was still anxious. Indeed, I reasoned to myself that worship that carries the name "Christian" is a response to a living reality in Jesus Christ, a response that requires faith and obedience. So I took partial comfort in the fact that I could at least pay attention to the rhythm of Pastor Imbundi's sermon even though it was spoken in Swahili. His text was a familiar one from Paul's letter to the Philippians:

> Whatever is true, whatever is honorable, whatever is just, whatever is pure, whatever is lovely, whatever is gracious, if there is any excellence, if there is anything worthy of praise, think about these things. What you have learned and received and heard and seen in me, do. (Phil. 4:8–9)

The mere recital of this familiar passage with its clear moral mandates eased my anxiety a bit. If, as St. Paul reminds us metaphorically, Christians see "through a glass darkly," it was my inability to understand what Pastor Imbundi was saying in his sermon that evoked the terror of the darkness for me. Moreover, I knew that the main "good" to come from any worship experience is the deepening of one's relationship with God and the covenant community of faith. Thoughts like this helped me concentrate on bits and pieces of the sermons; after all, worship is a place of vision and hope—a place where the blind see, the lame walk, the deaf hear, the weak find strength, and the oppressed find freedom and acceptance.

My theological training taught me that worship is not ours but "God's service in us." Through the acts of confession and sacrament we affirm what God has done and is doing in the world. The gift of worship is not in our hands alone. True worship functions in at least three ways: First, it gives centrality to the praise of God for "bringing us a mighty long ways," to use the language of traditional black religion. Second, worship builds solidarity in the community of faith. Third, worship enables us to remember our pilgrim identity as Christians as we toil, suffer, and respond to the needs of the poor and downtrodden in the world.

"Could it be," I wondered, "that the truth of the gospel story is rooted in such a vision of worship?" I tried to sort through this, arguing with myself as I sat in the pew. Nervously. . . . I continued to marvel at and ponder such lofty ideals and Christian values in an effort to relieve my anxiety. Undoubtedly we can do visioning like this to detach ourselves from the terror of the darkness of any moment.

Perhaps my real motivation here was to find a thread of security in my insecurity in worship—I really don't know. I *knew* instinctively that the people of St. Andrew's Episcopal Church believe as I do that we are one family in the commonwealth of Jesus Christ, in his life, death, and resurrection; and that God has a moral claim upon our lives to be keepers of justice and peace. But I still felt alone and an outsider. I felt out of place for I had been shaped by a different set of religious values, symbols, language, and habits that not only give me a vision of life but make me who I am. For better or worse, all I could honestly claim was, "I am a Christian"—and even that may be claiming too much.

A product of a middle-class Protestant church in America, and new to and naive about the complexity of indigenous African worship, I rapidly discovered—to my surprise—that many societies in Africa seem to lack what might be called a "civil religion," a unifying set of beliefs and customs, a shared memory or values capable of forming a basis for social solidarity. I dared to ponder the thought that many worshipers in St. Andrew's, sitting immediately behind me and across the aisle, could find in the Christian faith a liberating and unifying hope, radically open to the needs of the neighbors and the stranger in their midst. But I quickly cautioned myself not to think this way, for fear that it might be construed as too "western" or too "American" in character. Did not holy scriptures say, "Judge ye not"? Rather the true test of Christians is how we practice God's righteousness, love, and peace. These sorts of thoughts kept rushing through my mind as I sat for more than an hour, listening and trying to understand what was going on as Pastor Imbundi moved toward the end of his sermon. Yet, I still could not rid myself of uncomfortable feelings.

Suddenly, I saw a warm smile and heard a pleasant voice say, "Hey, can I interpret what's happening for you? I can tell you're new here and don't understand our worship." I quickly replied, "Oh, yes, you're right." He introduced himself, noticing the tense look on my face. "My name is Richard Kubi. I can help you." "Great," I whispered, my bottom lip quivering slightly. Richard spoke both Swahili and English. He nodded his head indicating that I should open the RSV that was in the wooden jacket on the back of the pew. And Richard began to interpret for me the last few minutes of Pastor Imbundi's sermon. Because he was so fluent in English, he could easily translate the sermon without drawing undue attention to us. Well, by then the first part of the worship was over, and all that remained was the celebration of Holy Communion.

"I saw that you were struggling," said Richard as we paused momentarily during the offering period. He had sensed my apprehension, anguish, and embarrassment. Richard gave a big smile and said, "Be of good cheer; communion will go much better. Don't forget the words from Philippians: 'Whatever is true . . . just . . . pure . . . lovely.' Think about these things." I pondered these things and more. Communion went by swiftly and worship at St. Andrew's was finally over. Afterward, I expressed deep thanks to Richard Kubi, who came to my rescue as a good Samaritan as I groped in the dark in that lonely pew. After the benediction, Pastor Imbundi warmly greeted all members and visitors at the rear of the church. As I walked down the steps of the church, I heard Richard joyfully exclaim, "Go my brother, John Lawson. Fare thee well!" Not uttering a further word, I continued to ponder the lingering questions, Had I really participated in worship? How do we welcome the stranger in our midst?

DISCUSSION NOTES

Tools of learning and group discussion, cases are vital expressions of universal human experience. I believe that they function in the life and faith of the church to shape our intellectual growth not only on critical issues of morality and culture but also on matters of worship and spirituality. The case before us involves the ambivalent feelings of an American missionary who inadvertently found himself in a new church and at a Swahili worship service. Discomfort, a sense of irony, and surprise greeted John Lawson, seemingly at every point in the worship.

Readers and discussion leaders may want to be particularly attentive to the polarity of John Lawson's feelings: wonderment and dis-ease, ecstasy and anger, cultural blindness, and embarrassment at that blindness. Many of his feelings were rooted in his identity as a child of Western society. One can proceed in this case by examining what it means and feels like to experience alternative expressions of Christian worship outside the orbit of American culture and social values. Perhaps we are guilty of a certain liturgical provincialism in the way we offer praise and expressions of adoration to God.

Another issue readers may wish to explore is the sort of ambivalence a person often feels when he or she is suddenly thrust into a minority status, as John Lawson was. An American missionary, John apparently felt the acute awkwardness of role reversal in his transition out of membership in the dominant social group. His culture shock came from his metamorphosis into a *minority* Christian in a strange land. Here, what I am trying to suggest for group discussion and theological reflection is simply the practical exercise of role-reversal. Ethically, we may also ask, How would you imagine and cope with the experience of Christian worship celebrated not in your own tradition or language?

It is also interesting to point out, in terms of this case, the gift of *hospitality* extended to John by Richard Kubi, a fellow worshiper at the Swahili service. In experiencing black Christian values in Africa, I was constantly amazed by the way the Kikuyu people show hospitality and love to the stranger. For example, when I first arrived in Kenya, East Africa, the Swahili words most commonly used were *jambo* and *harambee*. *Jambo* simply means "How are you?" or "Hello"; *harambe* connotes peoplehood, togetherness, and unity. These words easily filled the ordinary conversations between American missionaries and African Christians. Through these simple forms of greetings John Lawson was, undoubtedly, challenged to see and experience the worship of God in a different way. The narrative indicates that John's growth did not come without spiritual pain and agonizing. For African Christians, the gift of hospitality seems to be always tempered by a tough realism, captured in this Swahili proverb, Mgeni skiumbili; siku ya tatu mpe jembe! (Treat your guest as a guest for two days; but on the third give him a hoe.)

Ethical Approach

1. What is the role of the worshiping community with respect to the "stranger"?
2. What are the ethical requirements of Christian hospitality?
3. Can the practice of Christian love overcome language barriers? If so, how?

Issues for Reflection

1. Given the situation, were John Lawson's mixed feelings of awkwardness and anger justified? Understandable?
2. In a similar cross-cultural circumstance, what would you do as an individual?
3. What deeper issues are at stake in this case?

SUGGESTED READING

Baker, Benjamin S. *Feeding the Sheep: The Biblical Case for Ministry to Human-need*. Nashville: Broadman Press, 1985.

———. *Shepherding the Sheep: Pastoral Care in the Black Tradition*. Nashville: Broadman Press, 1983.

Carter, Harold A. *The Prayer Tradition of Black People*. Valley Forge, Penna.: Judson Press, 1976.

Goodwin, Bennie E. *Pray Right! Live Right! Reflections on the Lord's Prayer*. Downer's Grove, Ill.: Inter-Varsity Press, 1979.

Hastings, Adrian. "The Choice of Words for Christian Meanings in Eastern Africa." In *African Catholicism: Essays in Discovery*. London: SCM Press, 1989.

———. *Church and Mission in Modern Africa*. New York: Fordham University Press, 1967.

———. *A History of African Christianity 1950–1975*. Cambridge: Cambridge University Press, 1979.

Jones, A. M. *African Hymnody in Christian Worship*. Gwelo, Zimbabwe: Mambo Press, 1976.

Mbiti, John. "An African Views American Black Theology." In *Black Theology, A Documentary History 1966–1979*. Maryknoll, N.Y.: Orbis Books, 1979.

Nyamiti, Charles. *African Theology, Its Nature, Problems and Methods*. Eldoret, Kenya: Gaba Pastoral Institute, 1971.

————. *The Scope of African Theology*. Eldoret, Kenya: Gaba Pastoral Institute, 1973.

Pobee, John. *Toward an African Theology*. Nashville: Abingdon Press, 1979.

Thompson, Norma H., ed. *Religious Pluralism and Religious Education*. Birmingham, Ala.: Religious Education Press, 1988.

Washington, Preston R. *From the Pew to the Pavement*. Morristown, N.J.: Aaron Press, 1986.

————. *God's Transforming Spirit: Black Church Renewal*. Valley Forge, Penna.: Judson Press, 1988.

CASE

8

A DATE
WITH DESTINY

The young African minister Anthony Njoroge is well acquainted with the dangers and rewards of social struggle to improve the quality of life. He combines a kind of childlike innocence and deep religious faith. He is a man of bold Christian vision who seeks to practice what he preaches in the daily activities of village life. Most of his pastoral work is done with rural village people as they struggle to understand the meaning of Christian faith and its relevance in their everyday lives. For many Africans, religion and life are one. Religion seems to undergird the fabric of social life, and the force of religion is sometimes symbolized by the use of the Swahili term *harambee*, which means unity or pulling together. Poignantly direct, Anthony expressed his philosophy to me this way: "The message and the man must be one."

Who is Anthony Njoroge? Anthony is twenty-nine, the first born of James Kuria and Alice Wanjiku. He has six brothers and four sisters, Charles Nganga, Stephen Waweru, Arthur Kanyua, Peter Ndungu, George Ndungu, Duncan Mworia, Milkah Njeri, Helen Warjini, Margaret Wambui, and Ann Wairimu. Anthony is a medium-built black man, with a bold, revealing face. His dark brown eyes reveal a man full of life, warmth, and courage, on the one hand, yet one who is still slightly troubled by the turmoil and hurts of an uneven childhood, on the other.

Anthony is happily married to Janet Muthoni, who is thirty, and they are the proud parents of two children, Judy, 7, and Esther, 6. Anthony grew up in the village of Ngecha, which is located in the Kiambu District of the central province of Kenya. The population of this closeknit village community in the heart and soul of Kikuyuland is approximately 20,000. Many of the village people are agriculturalists, craftsmen, field workers, and artists. Increasingly, people migrate daily by foot and public transport to find work in nearby towns and cities. The average annual income of laborers in the Kiambu District is reportedly less than $400 per year. Accordingly, there is a constant struggle to find adequate food, clothing, shelter, health care, and safe drinking water; and the opportunity for a good education for children and young adults is elusive. Anthony was most fortunate as a person of faith, one "blessed by the gods of Kikuyuland," to finish Form Four, which means he has the Western equivalent of a high school diploma. Even more amazing, considering the difficulty of his youth, Anthony completed six and one-half additional years of education at area schools and Bible colleges.

But it was not only in his education that Anthony broke with cultural tradition. His faith journey would suggest that in that, too, he ran counter to what his culture expected. Anthony has held positions in his church and community—from Sunday school teacher to choir master, from music composer to service officer for the East African Christian Alliance, which is related to the International Council of Christian Churches. He is currently serving as pastor of the Limuru Baptist Fellowship, a small village church with about ninety-five regular members. His salary from the church is approximately 600 shillings per month, a meager salary, given the financial demands of his growing family. The family income is supplemented greatly by his wife, Janet, who works as an executive secretary in Nairobi. The story of this African minister is a chronicle of hope and stubborn courage amidst the crippling odds of his youth culture. But Anthony's chronicle of hope is also scarred by pitfalls and hurts that led to what he calls his "date with destiny."

Anthony's story is rooted in his childhood and his position as firstborn. As we sat and talked in the solitude of my study, I asked him, "In terms of your faith journey, what was the burden of being the firstborn?"

He replied, "As the firstborn, I had a lot of struggles. But being the firstborn also meant much to me, because for my mother I had to play the role of a father to my little brothers and sisters. Even though I was only a kid myself! . . . I had a special role to play in my family and with my mother, since, from as early as I can remember, my father had a drinking problem and didn't hold down a job on a regular basis. Now, because of him my mother had to go out to work on land (*shamba*) owned by someone else for only six shillings per day" [less than fifty cents]. Anthony continued, "As a family we didn't have much; we lived in a rural mud hut, with the sun as our source of light by day and an old thin blanket to ward off the damp and cold of the night. What meals we ate were mostly *mahindi* (maize), *namna ya ujimzito* (porridge), *kiazi* (pota-toes), and *a kuhusu mboga au mimea* (vegetables)."

I asked, "What was your mother like when you were a child?" Anthony responded, "I was raised in a Christian home (Baptist), and my mother was a devout Christian. She would take us to church where we would read the Bible a lot, and sing old gospel songs . . . Daddy didn't go with us much because of his drinking problem . . . It's strange to say, but I think his problem became for me my date with destiny . . . a time of trial and testing of faith."

"How, then, did your mother deal with the family situation?"

With a look of anguish, Anthony replied, "Those were real rough times for us in the family; I remember the time my mother was about to give birth to one of my younger sisters, and how she wanted daddy to be there so badly—just to help out and give support. But he was nowhere to be found . . . I think daddy was out drinking and having a good time. I remember him showing up several days later, acting as if nothing had happened. That really angered me and hurt my mother very much."

"As a woman of faith, how did your mother react; how did she feel?"

For a moment Anthony fell silent; he moved anxiously in the chair, crossing and uncrossing his legs. "Well, our mother was a strong Chris-tian woman who taught us not to fret about the way daddy was, but to have faith in God. I was so frustrated at the time that I just couldn't bring myself to accept what my mother was saying. Much later, I discovered that my mother read the Bible and prayed a lot, in order to silence the cries of her heart—because of daddy's problem and all. That was crushing for me . . . I didn't know that mama concealed the darkness of her pain that way. Finding that out forced me to question God, and how something like this could happen. Why do bad things happen to good people?"

By now, Anthony was sitting on the edge of his seat. His voice grew louder, like a great clap of thunder. Seconds later he calmed down, but his questions lingered on. I then asked, "Did your father work?" "Oh yes, he worked, but it was irregular. I believe that he cared for us in his own way; but there was hardly enough money, if any, to make ends meet as we lived cramped into our mud hut. When he did work, my father was a soil technician."

"As the firstborn and now as a pastor, how do you feel about all of this?" I asked. "Well, looking back, I see that the echo of my father's drinking brought me grief throughout my youth." He gazed at the ceiling and reflected on the gravity of the question, then continued, "Suddenly, there was a turning point in my life—I don't exactly recall how; I was seventeen years old then. But it was as though I could hear the voice of God, rising like a river, above the madness of the liquor bottle. Strangely, I no longer resented my father but felt sorry for him. It seems that God used the dread of this experience to call me into service."

"But how did you actually come to know Christ in your faith journey?" I asked. "In December of 1976, I was saved at an evangelistic meeting run under the auspices of the Grace Baptist Mission. Spiritually and emotionally, I was near the edge; I was at a point of crisis in my family; and, like my mother, I needed the word of the Lord God to help me through my problems. I had faith in myself enough to believe that whatever my problems, the Lord God would see me through."

"Then what?"

Anthony immediately broke into a warm smile, stood up and propped one arm on the edge of the bookshelf, and said, "I surrendered. I let go. I accepted Christ as my personal Savior. Then a funny thing happened: I accepted—almost like a revelation—that I couldn't make my father over! I was seized by the whole experience—and it sort of plunged me into the ministry. The voice of God came in part through daddy's drinking. I heard the echo of God's voice as my back was pressed to the wall of that bad experience."

Even now as Anthony looks at his toils and struggles, his desires and dreams as pastor of the Limuru Baptist Fellowship, a large portion of his self-understanding and identity is mirrored in these trying experiences with his father and mother. They were benchmarks in his faith journey as a minister of the gospel of Jesus Christ.

But, powerful as they were, these were not the only benchmarks. Still another force contributed to his identity and faith journey. During the early years of Anthony's Bible college experience, he came to understand firsthand the mixed impact of the missionary movement in Kenya. During his childhood in the village community of Ngecha, Anthony was taught that a "missionary was a saint," that everything missionaries taught represented God's will and was, therefore, good. One day at Bible college, a white missionary gave him a parttime job as a music assistant. As work and school progressed, Anthony began to trust the missionary who had came to the need of this poor, struggling African student out of a genuine sense of charity. But one day Anthony inadvertently discovered that this same missionary had written back to the Home Mission Board in the United States and falsely reported that he was helping at least twenty disadvantaged Africans to make it through school. In reality, the missionary was helping only one. "And guess who that was?" Anthony asked. The missionary then requested that the Home Mission Board send more money immediately because it was desperately needed to better propagate the gospel to the poor childlike natives of Kenya! In a fit of rage and moral indignation, Anthony stormed into the missionary's office and shouted, "You said you were my brother in Christ, and I wholeheartedly believed you . . . I trusted you . . . I honored your word that you would not lie, but now I've found you out!" Without allowing a response, he continued, "It seems that the teachers who come here as such loving missionaries are always holding us back, while at the same time pushing the juicy carrot out before our noses, as if we were only jackasses!"

Anthony's naivete was lost, and his confidence and trust in the school run by missionaries was shattered. His view of the nobility of the missionary movement was painfully altered. Today Anthony still agonizes over what the missionaries did to his land, a land of rich valleys and ridges, of sloping mountains and gushing streams that once gave so much life to the people in traditional African society.

Anthony now believes that, with the coming of the European missionaries, the peaceful, secure life of the villagers was drastically and permanently altered. He laments, "The missionaries came and condemned everything 'African,' because in their eyes Africa was a symbol of darkness and evil . . . Africa was the same as the *devil*—and the Christianity they taught us demanded that we chase the devil out." For Anthony, this was another date with destiny—a moment of awakening and testing—a conflict between conscience and desire. To be sure, Anthony is still haunted by many problems and concerns which he cannot control or even fully comprehend. He continues to wonder about God's purpose or role in his own ministry and work, his emerging family life, and the burden of his childhood even as he desperately tries to make sense out of the peaks and valleys of his own faith journey.

DISCUSSION NOTES

There are many complex issues in this case on the faith journey of Anthony Njoroge. It is important to point out that to push ahead speedily and come up with only a partial solution to the issues here would be ethically unwarranted. One approach that may be useful for discussion is role-playing. As difficult as it might seem, try to imagine yourself in Anthony's shoes.

In your critical analysis you might, for instance, use the popular approach of situation ethics, which begs the question, What is the most loving thing to do? How much would your own church tradition, Bible interpretation, and cultural experience shape the response you make to the dilemmas of the case?

In the course of "role-playing," try and identify two or three crucial issues that interest or puzzle you as a moral and honest Christian. First, you may focus on the conflicting meanings of being a "missionary" and follower of Christ in a foreign country. For example, a key issue in Anthony's moral struggle was cultural confusion, given the complex history of Christianity in Kenya, about the identity of the white missionary as "saint or deceiver."

Second, you may wish to probe the wider issue of blind loyalty to church hierarchy and authority. Implicitly, the struggles and experiences of Anthony Njoroge reflect, in part, this concern of how to be a faithful follower of Jesus Christ in whatever socio-cultural setting one might do ministry.

Third, I suspect that the problem of "land-grabbing" by the oppressing forces of colonialism and denominationalism during the period prior to Kenyan independence must weigh heavily in any understanding and discussion of Anthony's particular case and the world in which he was born.

Thus, we may consider the following concerns for discussion.

Ethical Approach

1. How would you likely respond to Anthony Njoroge's dilemma? Use the technique of role-playing to demonstrate. Someone must play the oppressor.
2. From the perspective of mission and evangelism, what would be your urging to people sent to foreign countries in the name of Jesus Christ?
3. What resources would you draw upon to better meet the needs of Alice Wanjiku, Anthony's mother?

Issues for Reflection

1. What do you think about Anthony's attitude toward his father?
2. Were Anthony's feelings toward the white missionary morally justified?
3. What other concerns do you find pertinent in this case?

SUGGESTED READING

Barrett, David B., et al., eds. *Kenya Churches Handbook: The Development of Kenyan Christianity, 1498–1973*. Kisumu, Kenya: Evangel Publishing House, 1973.

Boesak, Allan A. *Farewell to Innocence*. Maryknoll, N.Y.: Orbis Books, 1977.

Chu, Daniel, and E. Skinner. *A Glorious Age in Africa*. New York: Zenith Books, 1965.

DeGruchey, John. *Cry Freedom*. Maryknoll, N.Y.: Orbis Books, 1986.

Dickson, Richard D. *To Set at Liberty the Oppressed*. Geneva: World Council of Churches, 1975.

Fluker, Walter E. *They Looked for a City*. Lanham, Md.: University Press of America, 1989.

Jones, Major J. *The Color of God*. Macon, Ga.: Mercer University Press, 1987.

Mazrui, Ali A. *The Africans: A Triple Heritage*. Boston: Little, Brown & Co., 1986.

Mbiti, John S. *African Religions and Philosophy*. New York: Anchor Books, 1970.

Ngugi, Wa Thiong'o. *Writers in Politics*. London: Heinemann Educational Books, 1981.

Thomas, Tony, ed. *Black Liberation and Socialism*. New York: Pathfinder Press, 1974.

9

IS INTIMACY
POSSIBLE?

"It frightens, saddens, and troubles me that in today's society so many young, up-and-coming African Christians seem not to value the old ways too much," exclaimed the Reverend Philemon Usuwana Mapuranga, a professor at United Theological College in Harare, Zimbabwe. Mr. Mapuranga, forty-seven, is an ordained minister in the United Church of Christ.

The issue of this case is not simply how to understand the "new" in light of the "old" or the "old" in light of the "new." Nor is it simply the cliché "generation gap," a phrase which has received more than its just due in Western society. In Philemon's thought, struggles, and faith experiences, the issue has been more basic than that. The issue that seemed most to trouble him as our interview unfolded was not, ironically, white versus black, apartheid versus a free society, oppression versus liberation, or any combination of ideological opposites. Rather, we spent most of our time discussing the relative absence or presence of community—and whether that hurts or enhances what it means to be both African and Christian.

In the struggles and faith experiences of Philemon, the issue of community is essentially the question of intimacy. Given the shifting boundaries of modern African culture, I invited Philemon to ponder the question, Is intimacy possible? He responded initially by suggesting that human beings mirror faith in God in many ways. Intimacy is one of these ways. "Intimacy is the language human beings must use to restore our fellowship with God and creation. Christ was about intimacy as he established a new foundation by which we relate to one another as persons." And in his view, Christ is calling African Christians and all people to do nothing less.

In Philemon's self-understanding and his story of faith, the ideas of intimacy and community are one and the same. In his view, these ideas of intimacy and community—one that they are—seem to create certain problems for Christians in modern African society. As the drama of this case unfolded there was, on the one hand, much to celebrate and laugh about. And on the other, there was much to feel morally disturbed about. If the Swahili proverb is true that "Dry bread in one's own home is better than good meat in some other place," then he does not believe that one's cultural home should be blindly left behind—as is being done by too many contemporary African Christians who believe the illusion that life is better "in some other place." The "dry bread" is a metaphor for togetherness or community, the center around which things come together. According to Philemon, many young Africans are confused about community, about the center of life, about the values that hold together the center—if indeed those values any longer work. Let us now take a closer look at Philemon U. Mapuranga.

Behind Philemon's strong physique and dark brown eyes is a quiet but self-confident man full of warmth, spontaneity, spiritual centeredness, and a deep passion for community. Philemon is happily married to Ethel Mapuranga; they are the proud parents of four children, Chipo, 16, Austakaare, 14, Moses, 12, and Selina, 10. Active in community issues related to pastoral care and theology, the Mapuranga family currently lives on the campus of United Theological College, where he teaches pastoral theology and advanced courses in counseling. Philemon's professional identity has been punctuated with achievement and struggle.

He received his primary and secondary education largely at missionary schools in Zimbabwe (formerly Rhodesia). He also did graduate studies abroad in theology and counseling. Prior to his appointment as lecturer at United, Philemon had served at various posts in the United Church of Christ of Zimbabwe, especially working to relate effective clinical insights to the concrete problems of modern African life. He insisted, "Absolute faithfulness to a sense of community is the thing most needed as our society experiences rapid social change and globalization." During our conversation, Philemon returned time and time again to the question of community, which he called "intimacy," and to the question, Given the modern forces at work in Africa today, is community, or intimacy, really possible without recovery of the storytelling tradition? Slowly but surely, this had become the fundamental question that deeply concerned Philemon relative to the issues of faith and liberation. He believed that the simple facts of modern African life—the way people speak, act, and behave in church and society—often work against the values of intimacy, sharing, storytelling, and compassion. "Even in our churches, people today find it hard to relate to one another, to truly speak their minds, to share what's bothering them, to tell their stories . . . I find this difficult to accept and a flaw in our character that's, no doubt, traceable to a neglect of tradition and an erosion of oral customs," he explained. In the interview, we spent a long time together, largely over tea and cookies, in the home of the principal of the college, pondering these concerns in the lifestyle and work habits of contemporary Christians in African society.

As Philemon discussed his own faith story, I was struck by his ethical and historical sensitivity to those early experiences that helped to shape his character. An energetic young man, Philemon grew up in the District of Chipinge which is located in the Manica Province in the Republic of Zimbabwe. In this traditional village community of 500 people, there was much to do and say. For one thing, farmers did not idle their time away. They planted maize, peas, beans, and millet. Women and children patiently worked the land, hoping and praying, without cease, for adequate rainfall and sunshine to assure a good harvest each year.

Around the flourishing fields and crops, rows of houses dotted the rural landscape. Mothers and children sang joyful melodies and listened to the stories told by the elders at evening-tide, giving life to each other in the process. As Philemon recalled his childhood, the farmers did not have much in terms of economic security. Indeed, many actually earned less than $50 per month for their labor. "Working with the soil and herding cows and goats did not yield much money in those days, but many of us had something inside that money couldn't buy, that guns couldn't destroy, that technology couldn't control . . . We had emotional security; we had elders and grandmothers who cared for us and reminded us of the stories and old tales that keep us out of trouble." With a look of joy, amazement, and excitement beaming from his face, Philemon further recounted, "The main thing I remember about growing up as a Zulu is not the lack of money but the feeling of emotional security that I got from my family and community . . . This is the intimacy that we somehow have lost today as we see young boys and girls grow up in Africa . . . As Zulus, we had a sense of belonging back then; but today, people are not ready for intimacy." Like many of the ideas, sayings, or tales peculiar to a particular tradition, the concept of intimacy in the faith journey of Philemon is not primarily a private concept. Rather, in the context of his faith experience, the concept of intimacy, even the lack of it, is part of the "shared wisdom of the community."

To illustrate this concept, Philemon told a story of a dance once done in his community; the dance is *muchongoyo*. The muchongoyo dance involved a group of eight children between the ages of nine and twelve. As bystanders looked on with excitement and admiration, the eight children would form a circle in the center of the village. In a playful and rhythmic manner, they would clap their hands and stomp their feet three times as drums, cymbals, and other musical instruments echoed in the background. Between each three claps, someone would shout out the name of a noble warrior or elder; then other village onlookers would join in. The muchongoyo dance would go on for hours as everyone became engrossed in the activity and provided explosions of roaring applause for each other. The ritualistic dance would continue until the dance partners could no longer recite names. Philemon believes that such expressions of fun and amusement can go far toward recovering a genuine sense of intimacy, and providing each person with a glimpse into new forms of togetherness that are rooted in their own tradition and customs.

Of course, Philemon's childhood and early teens were not all a matter of fun and games. He had bouts with sickness, poverty, and hardship. In 1947, when he was nine years old, he became seriously ill with pneumonia, so ill that his mother became gravely worried that he might die. One late afternoon before dusk, his mother carried Philemon to an open tent-revival meeting. There, under the open sky and in the midst of the evangelistic fervor, Philemon recalled, a grassroots preacher named Rubuen Mitisi urged him to come up to the front row for prayer. "Looking back, I can think about it now, but then my lips were quivering and my knees were shaking badly. I was scared, but my mother came with me; there were tears in my mother's eyes, and fear in my own heart—yet that didn't stop us. Suddenly, evangelist Mitisi, whom I had never seen before—or since—burst into singing "Amazing Grace" and before I realized it, everybody was up on their feet shouting and praying aloud . . . and I don't remember what happened next, except when I left that meeting, my illness was gone. They prayed and I was healed."

Although Philemon said that he had not had much faith or confidence in God before the revival meeting, he believed that the prayers of the community actually healed him. From that point on, he read the Bible on a regular basis and believed in the power of God's healing grace. At the root of his belief today is the conviction that the African understanding of God allows room for direct "divine intervention" into the daily lives of ordinary faithful people. This was one of the primary moral values that shaped his character as a young man.

The idea of the dignity of work was another crucial moral value that forged Philemon's identity and character. For him, work is both a means of creative self-expression and a basic clue to faith and to understanding a God who commands each person to "work out their own salvation with fear and trembling before the Lord." A practical side of this principle was demonstrated in the hard work required just in order to survive the ups-and-downs of rural life. Philemon himself had to work on a tea plantation—usually from sunup to sundown—to supplement the family income during hard times. "It didn't feel right for me at the time," said Philemon, "But later I came better to understand the wisdom of my father's words, 'Be not afraid of work, for work is good and natural.' " Needless to say, to a young lad, tedious laboring from morning till evening felt neither good nor natural. But with the perspective of time, Philemon recognizes the valuable lesson he learned about work, a lesson that has stayed with him. He expressed it in the following manner, "In the place where I grew up, people would call you bad names and even crack your head if you didn't want to work; in our family, we affirmed the dignity of work as a value that sustains the spirit of community among the people who lived in our district of Chipinge. But now things are changing so rapidly in our society, many folks are leaving behind these values that served us so well in the past . . . That bothers me and gives my heart pain."

Toward the end of the interview, Philemon expressed mixed feelings about the future, in light of increasing unemployment, crime, drug abuse, and social drinking in many African countries, as people move from rural to urban areas searching for a better way of life. As a teacher and counselor, he wonders about the continuing erosion of traditional moral and spiritual values. And he wonders how ministers and leaders who now serve in African churches will deal with these complex problems that further undermine community or intimacy.

What struck me the most about Philemon's faith journey was not his anxiety or fear over the modern problems African Christians face—pressing and critical as they are—but his spiritual heritage and his longing for the intimacy once joyfully shared by fathers and sons, mothers and daughters, sisters and brothers in African village life. I was touched by his deep sense of longing and loss and his hope that all people—Christian and non-Christian alike—will recover the genius of their own spiritual roots. His words linger in my mind: "Spiritual roots are essentially moral." I sensed from Philemon's story that to him this was both the burden and promise of the vision wrapped up in the word "intimacy." It was as though Philemon was actually saying to me—perhaps at a more profound religious level—the words of the prophet Jeremiah, "O Lord, renew our days of old!"

DISCUSSION NOTES

In regular group discussion we may observe the drama of this case as expressive of three important themes in contemporary African life: (1) the struggle for "intimacy" in the midst of rapid social change in developing African nations; (2) the impact of early childhood experiences on identity and character; and (3) faith as a tool in healing and the renewal of Christian community. Of course there are other crucial issues and religio-cultural themes here which deserve attention. And moral reasoning or reflection is appropriate in areas of one's own interest and experience.

The drama of this case involves the life and faith pilgrimage of Philemon Usuwana Mapuranga, an ordained minister in the United Church of Christ in Harare, Zimbabwe. Reading this case study, one is struck by the idea of intimacy among African Christians as a way of imaging the totality of God's presence with us as we confront the trials of life. Closely related to Philemon's concern for intimacy is the importance of storytelling as a shaping force in his life and his early faith pilgrimage. Elders of his village recited stories of faith, courage, and moral struggle that helped to shape Philemon's social character and worldview. The ethic of hardwork outside of the home and joyful storytelling in the home formed two dialectical poles that gave shape to Philemon's self-understanding as a minister of the gospel of Jesus Christ. As a morally sensitive person, he deeply laments the gradual demise of what he calls traditional "oral customs." In analysis of this case, we may wish to explore how brothers and sisters in church communities in the West understand "oral customs" and their import for faith affirmation and the transformation of social life.

Philemon's lament about the loss of intimacy is heard throughout this case. He argues that modern African life seems to lack most the security that comes from knowledge of God's presence in one's own indigenous community. This case expresses the view that, for African Christians sensitive to social tradition, intimacy is not about chasing Western values. Rather it is about (1) God's sustaining presence among suffering people; and (2) feeling culturally at home. The Swahili proverb put the matter this way: "Dry bread in one's own home is better than good in some other place." Perhaps North American Christians may be able to draw a lesson from this African proverb in terms of how we perceive global mission and the proclamation of the gospel of Jesus Christ in distant places. I suspect that cultural integrity is the issue as Christians witness to the power of the gospel to set women and men free: Western missionaries often have real difficulty adapting to and respecting the cultural integrity of African people. In this case, we may also wish to ask, as a discussion starter, How can we affirm the value of cultural integrity when we lose our sense of community?

Ethical Approach

1. What can North American Christians learn from the African concept of intimacy?
2. What is the church's task in light of the need for community and intimacy?
3. List five ways to enhance a sense of community in your own church or neighborhood.

Issues for Reflection

1. What are your points of agreement or disagreement with Philemon's attitude on the demise of so-called traditional values?
2. What sort of problems can result from the absence of intimacy in family, church, or society?
3. What insights do you bring from your own personal experiences on the question of intimacy?

SUGGESTED READING

Chernoff, John Miller. *African Rhythm and African Sensibility: Aesthetics and Social Action in African Musical Idioms*. Chicago: University of Chicago Press, 1979.

Collins, Robert O., ed. *Problems in African History*. Englewood Cliffs, N.J.: Prentice-Hall, 1968.

Diallo, Yaya, and Michell Hall. *African Wisdom Teachings*. Rochester, Vt.: Destiny Books, 1989.

Diop, Cheikh Anta. *Black Africa: The Economic and Cultural Basis for a Federated State*. Chicago: Lawrence Hill Books, 1987.

Fanon, Frantz. *Toward the African Revolution*. New York: Grove Press, 1988.

Howe, Russell W. *Black Africa: From the Colonial Era to Modern Times*. New York: Walker & Co., 1966.

Lebacqz, Karen. *Justice in an Unjust World*. Minneapolis: Augsburg Publishing House, 1987.

Mandela, Nelson. *No Easy Walk to Freedom*. Nairobi: Heinemann Educational Books, 1988.

Markovitz, Irving Leonard. *Studies in Power and Class in Africa*. New York: Oxford University Press, 1987.

Rodney, Walter. *How Europe Underdeveloped Africa*. Washington, D.C.: Howard University Press, 1982.

Turnbull, Colin M. *The Mountain People*. New York: Simon & Schuster, 1972.

CASE
10

CHILDREN OF APARTHEID

The green jeep, with its bright flashing light, sped through the dark and winding streets of Soweto, headed for a small squatter tenement house. Four officers armed with pistols and automatic weapons were in the jeep. It was very early, three o'clock in the morning. Pulling up to a small frame house, two of the officers, neatly dressed in military uniforms, walked briskly and in unison up the steps and knocked forcefully upon the door several times. In a moment a dim light illuminated the porch and the door opened a crack. "Who's there?" inquired a voice from inside. "Officers of the law!" shouted the men in a commanding tone. With a fear-filled voice, the man inside the house responded, "Sir, what do you want at this time of night? What can I do for you?" "Open up! Open up!" thundered the officers. The door swung wide and opened. The officers entered and spoke in an intimidating manner. There was tension and urgency in their voices as they said, "Your son, Kwesi, is under arrest for participating in an unauthorized school demonstration. Where is he?"

Stunned and baffled, the father, Jesse Mushete, suggested, "Excuse me, sir, but you must be mistaken."

"Oh no! There's no mistake, the boy must come with us immediately," ordered the officers. The father shook his head No but to no avail, as one of the officers stepped forth and nodded for the boy. Jesse Mushete instinctively knew that one thing he could not do in this violence-torn neighborhood was forcefully to resist the law. Even though the officers did not produce an arrest warrant, he reluctantly handed over his son, Kwesi, to them. The four officers sped off in the darkness and chill of the night, down a long, narrow, paved road toward the local police station.

"Where are you taking me?" asked Kwesi. "You'd better shut up, boy, if you know what's good for you!" shouted one of the officers. "I'm not afraid. I just want to know what's the problem," said the youngster. Suddenly, a large, thick, steel-plated, leather-covered nightstick was violently pressed against Kwesi's neck. "I told you to shut up, I mean shut up!" threatened one of the officers. But Kwesi refused and said again that he had done nothing wrong. The officer driving the jeep suddenly slammed on his brakes, pulled over to the side of the road, and beat the youngster into submission.

Once at the station, Kwesi was booked for curfew violations and unauthorized participation in a student strike. He was held in detention for three weeks, and was not allowed to see his family or friends. Kwesi was not alone in jail but was one of twenty-eight students and children of Soweto who had been picked up and held by the local police for school demonstrations. While in detention, Kwesi protested that he was innocent and had done no wrong. From that first evening, he pleaded with the chief officer, "Sir, let me call or see my parents. I'm hurt and this small, damp, musty jail cell is driving me up a wall!" "Just forget it," remarked the chief officer bluntly. "You rebellious, dirty youngsters need to be taught that you can't go around breaking the law. You ain't gonna better yourselves by demonstrations and school strikes. That only leads to more trouble and violence." In a patronizing manner, the chief asked, "Do you kids really know what's best for you?" "Dignity is best!" Kwesi briskly replied. "We'll teach you about dignity with the night stick," chuckled the officer arrogantly. With perspiration falling from his forehead, Kwesi said, "You mean submission. We'll never stop until we get our freedom!" Enraged, the officer was silent and uneasy for a moment. Breaking the silence and giving vent to his anger, he barked, "Enough of that! Or else . . . !"

The bruises on Kwesi's tall, frail body, acquired enroute to the local police station, painfully reminded him what the "else" meant. There he sat helpless, in jail, traumatized by events he was powerless to change. Later, after the three weeks of detention had passed, he would tell his father, "The detention was nothing less than a nightmare—constant chaos, harassment, and the threat of violence. The three weeks seemed like eternity."

The four officers who had arrested Kwesi later discovered that he was at the scene of the student demonstration but had not participated in it. Not surprisingly, they did not report the fact that Kwesi was unjustly detained for three weeks. Four of the other school-age children held in detention were hospitalized, and one suffered permanent brain damage as a result of repeated blows to the head administered by a police officer. The officer in question denied the brutality and alleged that the student had accidentally slipped and struck his head while in detention.

Obviously, even though unjustly held, Kwesi was a "lucky one"; he managed—though wracked with pain and morally outraged—to be reunited with his family and to return to school the following week. Meanwhile, the student demonstrations and class strikes continued. A growing minority of students, disenchanted with school policy over the use of indigenous language and curfew, openly and illegally protested. Kwesi was not yet a part of this growing minority. He had already been through a lot. His moral dilemma intensified as conflicting thoughts invaded his mind: Will dignity or freedom come by me remaining on the sideline? Knowing his parents' feelings, he weighed the issues: Should I participate in school demonstrations? What is the cost of dignity or freedom? As a Christian, what am I to do? He knew that there was a lot at stake, not just for him personally but for his family and the entire community. Although his father, Jesse, had a moderately well-paying job as a worker in the mines, he had never finished high school and had had to work at odd jobs, long hours into the night, to feed his six children—four girls and two boys—and provide housing for them. Mr. Mushete's job at the mine was "good," relatively speaking, compared with his previous work history. So Kwesi felt some obligation, then, not to do anything that would reflect poorly on his father or threaten his employment situation.

But Kwesi also felt strongly about the immorality of apartheid. He asked his father the disturbing question, "Why do whites treat us so meanly in our own country?" With a deep look of concern on his face, the father replied, "Well, son, I tell you . . . hatred and fear sometimes make would-be decent people do mean and evil things . . . I don't know, but it's strange how some folks fool themselves and believe they are better than others. God made us all equal, but some folks come to feel that they are more and we are less. That's the evil that prejudice does; it affects your mind and prevents you from seeing things straight . . . All they know to do is to react in violence and fear. But somehow our day of justice will come, and all of the world will see it—for God is on the side of people who suffer for what's right."

Kwesi found hope in his father's words, but his fear and anxiety about what he should do remained. Ironically, it is in South Africa that you find the greatest number of Christians per kilometer. It is in South Africa where the majority of people, largely blacks and coloreds, are still denied full participation in the political and economic life of the society—despite recent changes in the government which led to the celebrated release of Nelson Mandela. The South African government, by virtue of its apartheid system, has unlimited power to punish demonstrators at will, to put down school strikers with brute force, and to rule over the black population without allowing blacks any real say in creating the laws to which they are subjected. Children of apartheid are innocent victims of a world not of their own making.

With this social climate as background, Kwesi is desperately struggling to clarify his own moral dilemma. Should he openly shout "Liberation!" as countless others have done? He knows the costly price many have already paid for dignity: many workers have lost much needed jobs; wanderers and migrants have been banned; social activists have been exiled or left to rot in jail; Bantustans have been socially isolated; black and white university students have suffered police brutality; church leaders have been attacked and persecuted; and hundreds of people, including innocent children, have been shot dead in the streets. Reflecting on all this tragedy—and also on the hopes—Kwesi is deeply aware of the high cost of dignity and freedom. Yet, only he can decide what he will do.

He reasoned to himself, "The issue is not whether I stand for or against apartheid. That's already decided; I'm certainly against the evils of apartheid. Rather, my dilemma is—What form should my stand take? What wounds will I, or my family suffer?" Anxiety came over Kwesi as he came face to face with these questions. "Frankly, I feel afraid inside, but I know I must do something. Yet I am unsure if taking part in a demonstration is the best way for me," he lamented.

Suddenly, the expression on his face became tense and visibly pained. Tugging nervously at his ragged shirt sleeve, Kwesi cried, "Daddy, Daddy, why are we acting like scared prisoners in our own schools? Something is wrong here in Soweto. We're all victims—the whites, the blacks, the coloreds—in this nightmare system of apartheid." As he leaned forward Kwesi's voice trailed off into a whisper. "Daddy, you always taught us that 'God is love,'" to love everybody. . . . I hate the awful things I see. I hate the school, this violent place and all it's doing to us! . . . If God is love, why has God allowed this evil and suffering to continue?"

Jesse grasped Kwesi's hands and said, "Well, it ain't God's fault, son."

"Then whose fault is it, Daddy? Whose fault is it?" Words did not come from Jesse. All that came was a terrifying silence.

111

DISCUSSION NOTES

It is easy for people in Western society to assume that all parents can offer their children at least three things: protection, potency, and nurturing love. For Christians and many other people the world over, these basic elements are often taken for granted and regarded as the moral requisites of a healthy family life. Now, in this case, involving a South African father, Jesse Mushete, and his son Kwesi, no such easy assumption can be made about middle-class family virtues. Black children and their parents in South Africa have no real protection against the nightmare of police brutality, detention, violence, and death. Obviously, real fear permeates this situation, in which a young teenager was snatched from his home late at night, taken to a local police station, and held for three weeks. But, balancing the terror, we find hope and stubborn courage also present here—to be used as Kwesi chooses, but not without deep pain and suffering, in the attempt to achieve dignity over the crippling degradation of apartheid. Ultimately, Kwesi himself endured the nightmare of being jailed and was returned to his family and school three weeks after his arrest. He was a "lucky one." Undoubtedly, the issue of student demonstrations and class strikes conducted in the interests of authentic freedom and the right to cultural expression is a deep moral problem and concern. What is the cost of true freedom and the right to cultural expression? Theologically, we are compelled to ask all Christians, What is the cost of discipleship in a situation where children are crushed by the police force and the immoral use of power? Can we see the loving image of God in the faces of the children of apartheid?

Those in small groups in church and community may wish to discuss this case by role-playing. In your own home, church, or community, parents and practitioners of the Christian faith can structure learning sessions that carry American children and adults on an imaginary journey to South Africa. For example, what would "our" children say and do to children of South Africa—black or white—given the opportunity of face-to-face dialogue? What sort of games would they play with each other? What gifts or common experiences would they share? What can adults and parents learn from children who have been scarred by fear, social violence, and oppression? For Christians, what is the most loving and caring thing to do? These sorts of practical questions and concerns may appeal to some people discussing this case.

In the broader geo-political sense, Africa today is constantly in the news. The headlines in major newspapers the world over about hunger and malnutrition in Ethiopia and continued racial unrest and oppression in South Africa have underscored the importance of this continent. Modern technology and communication have, for better or worst, brought the disturbing social, political, and economic problems of Africa right into our living rooms.

Africa, as a continent, as part of the world, carries a big question in its heart. And this question is also a question *about* the rest of the world. A litany of questions have been raised by morally concerned persons: When will the dawn of true justice appear? When will the light of freedom shine? When will crying, hunger, and violence cease? When will the twin scandals of benevolent exploitation and tribalism be laid aside? When will the nations of the world make room for the sons and daughters of Africa to stand on equal footing? When will the children smile again?

The gospel of Jesus Christ and the tug of conscience require all faithful people of the church to think about, even agonize over, these questions. But the burden of finding real answers and solutions will not come easily.

Many worthwhile resources exist today that will enhance our understanding and theological discussion. One such resource is *The Unquestionable Right to Be Free*, edited by Itomeleng J. Mosala and Buti Tlhagale, which takes a hard look at the prophetic role of black theology in the historic struggle of the oppressed for freedom and human dignity in South Africa. Reflecting theologically on South African suffering, Mosala and Tlhagale identify four historical phases of black struggle in South Africa:

1. The "Khoisan phase," the initial clash of economic and cultural interests between the indigenous people and the early white settlers (the term "Khoisan" refers collectively to "Hottentots" and "Bushmen").

2. The "tribalistic phase," which refers to the armed clash between African people in the Eastern Cape and the encroaching white colonial forces during the eighteenth and early nineteenth centuries. The tragic result of this was the loss of land by black people and their subordination as dependent wage laborers.

3. The "nationalistic phase," beginning in the first decade of the twentieth century, which pointed toward the era of black national unity, in which the politics of moderation and integration led only to token constitutional reform.

4. The "black consciousness phase," in which the old politics of moderation between blacks and whites disappeared, and the festering sore of apartheid was laid bare for the world over to see. Under this

new banner of black consciousness, the ultimate goal of the black struggle—no matter what the cost—is liberation from all forms of oppression.

Ethically sensitive persons who read this case may also see it as a microcosm of the larger fabric of social life in South Africa. For children, parents, and common laborers alike, the fight for freedom and human dignity continues in South Africa. And the Christian community of faith is accountable always for its words and deeds. The proverbial words of South African theologian Allan Boesak strike me as especially relevant to this case:

> We will go before God to be judged, and God will ask us, "Where are your wounds?" And we will say, "We have no wounds." And God will ask, "Was nothing worth fighting for?"

Ethical Approach

1. In your view, who are the real victims of apartheid in a world come of age?
2. What are the practical requirements of the biblical imperative to "love mercy and do justice" in situations of oppression?
3. Are nations, as well as individuals, accountable to God for the work of social justice or injustice?

Issues for Reflection

1. What parallels do you see between Kwesi's dilemma and the struggle for dignity and human rights in other parts of the world? In your own church community or neighborhood?
2. What can be done by churches and concerned people to eliminate oppression and injustice in whatever form it takes?
3. How would you likely handle the dynamic between Kwesi and his father, Jesse?

SUGGESTED READING

Adams, Herbert. *Modernizing Racial Domination: The Dynamics of South African Politics*. Berkeley: University of California Press, 1971.

Bigo, Pierre. *The Church and the Third World Revolution*. Maryknoll, N.Y.: Orbis Books, 1974.

Boesak, Allan. *Farewell to Innocence*. Maryknoll, N.Y.: Orbis Books, 1986.

Bunting, Brian. *The Rise of the South African Reich*. New York: Penguin Books, 1964.

deGruchy, John. *Cry Justice*. Maryknoll, N.Y.: Orbis Books, 1986.

Fanon, Frantz. *Toward the African Revolution*. New York: Grove Press, 1988.

Goba, Bonganjalo. *An Agenda for Black Theology: Hermeneutics for Social Change*. Johannesburg, South Africa: Skotaville Publishers, 1988.

Hastings, Adrian. *African Christianity*. New York: Seabury Press, 1976.

Mandela, Nelson. *No Easy Walk to Freedom*. Nairobi, Kenya: Heinemann Educational Books, 1988.

Moore, Basil, ed. *The Challenge of Black Theology in South Africa*. Atlanta, Ga.: John Knox Press, 1974.

Mosala, Itumeleng, and Buti Tlhagale. *The Unquestionable Right to Be Free*. Maryknoll, N.Y.: Orbis Books, 1986.

Mzimela, Sipo E. *Apartheid: South African Nazism*. New York: Vantage Press, 1983.

Villa-Vicencio, Charles, ed. *Theology and Violence: The South African Debate*. Grand Rapids: Wm. B. Eerdmans, 1987.

CASE

11

NEVER STOP
CLIMBING

"We Are Climbing Jacob's Ladder" is an old Negro spiritual that had a strange influence on me when I was a child," said Pastor William Gillespie as we sat in his spacious church study and mused on his self-understanding of faith and liberation. Bill Gillespie has served as pastor of the Cote Brilliante Presbyterian Church for over thirty years. The position has been more than employment for this energetic man of vision and toil; it has been a depot for community outreach and compassion in the dark ghetto of North St. Louis. The perception of ministry as community involvement is not a strange one for Pastor Gillespie—for each day to his church's door the voiceless ones of the community "come knocking and crying," as he says. Such programs and projects as food for the hungry, shelter for the homeless, education for the mentally handicapped, day care, meals on wheels, karate and physical fitness classes, scouting, and youth achievement reflect the scope of his ministry in the community. These have been the ways by which Pastor Gillespie has attempted to respond to the voiceless ones who often lodge on the doorstep of the church. "Climbing Jacob's ladder must include the homeless, the locked out, and the crying ones," he says. "These folks test our faith as a Christian community."

In the life story of Bill Gillespie, faith and liberation take many forms. Providing a ministry of outreach and compassion is one of the many ways this African-American preacher has worked to empower those locked out in our society. In Gillespie's view, the church in the black community must be the "earthen vessel" that enables the marginal ones to find Jacob's ladder. As he observed, "The black church is the only earthen vessel sailing in the turbulent sea of the ghetto that black folks fully own." Partial to the irony of God's divine arithmetic, Gillespie is a key figure in interpreting the storms that rage upon the sea of black community life in America.

William G. Gillespie was born in Knoxville, Tennessee. He has been happily married to Martha Cox for many years, and they are the parents of three children, a daughter, Vendetta Lambert, and two sons, William Edward and Harry Gillespie. Even though he grew up on the "other side of the tracks," Gillespie is adamant in his view that the people in east Tennessee were far ahead of the state as a whole on the issues of social justice and social progress among blacks and whites. Describing his childhood in Knoxville, Gillespie exclaimed, "I was born in what you might say to be a hillbilly town, with loads of country music and downhome customs and all the rest. Actually, we had good relationships as far as the races were concerned . . . There was a difference in the folks from east Tennessee . . . My father finished high school and worked at the bus station and got along well with whites and blacks. My brother and I worked there, too, but daddy wanted more than that for us."

What was commonplace, said Bill, in the Gillespie family—in fact, in his neighborhood—was the basic belief that "you have to get a good education in order to get ahead, especially if you're 'colored,' as the old folks used to say." Beyond that, two other beliefs passed on to him by his parents, Matt and Virginia Gillespie, lodged in Bill's heart: "Fear God" and "Love God." Bill Gillespie highlighted the practical side of these beliefs by telling the story of how, when bad weather was approaching, his mother would gather all of the children together in one room. "My mother didn't allow us to do anything in times of stormy weather," Bill recalled. "She would tell us that a storm was the work of Almighty God and that whenever God worked in nature, we had to stop doing whatever we happened to be doing—singing, playing, studying; it didn't matter, everything had to stop because God was showing his mighty hand!" These sorts of early childhood experiences left their mark upon Bill's character.

His mother, Virginia, a faithful member of the Church of God, was a pentecostal. He remembers spending long hours with her in church on Sunday mornings. The opportunity to visit his mother's church was always greeted by young Bill with deep enthusiasm because there the faithful would testify about God's goodness and would "speak in tongues." His father's Baptist religion seemed better suited to Bill's religious temperament. Bill was especially fond of Mrs. Walker, a civic worker and an outstanding Bible teacher at the Paine Avenue Baptist

Church in Knoxville, who inspired him to study scripture daily and to learn more about God's liberating activity with oppressed people. It was at the church that Mrs. Walker taught Bill and the other children about "God's freeing power from the yoke of bondage, and about faith in your own gifts and abilities." There were other luminaries in his childhood, people who positively influenced his character. One was Fannie Clay, a civil rights worker, who helped to shape Bill's awareness and sense of social responsibility. The black spiritual, "Go Down Moses" was the sort of spiritual that renewed the fire of faith and hope in Bill's heart. This particular black spiritual was also a theme song of a popular radio program in his community. It spoke of inspiration and freedom and added to Bill's critical understanding of the importance of Christian ministry in urban society.

In times of crisis, Bill always referred to certain songs and experiences which served as sources of personal strength. For instance, songs such as "Go Down Moses," "Amazing Grace," and "Where He Leads Me" seem to function as a source of renewal and enablement in Bill's personal life. Another example of this lay in his decision to enter the Christian ministry. After graduation from high school and Knoxville College, Bill had made plans to attend medical school in Nashville. But then he was invited to be Youth Day speaker at the Paine Avenue Baptist Church. To his surprise, his message was received enthusiastically. In fact, his speech was so well received that he decided, then and there, that the Christian ministry was his calling, not medicine. He enrolled at Johnson C. Smith Seminary and became a Presbyterian pastor. Bill was then given the challenge of ministering to the hearts and souls of the blacks in North St. Louis.

Not content with one theological degree, the B.D., Bill went on to earn two additional degrees, the S.T.M. and the D.Min in order to better equip himself in service to the voiceless ones in community. Yet, in his character and faithfulness to his calling, Bill Gillespie's thoughts appear never to be that far from his mother's admonition to him: "Go with Jesus as you climb Jacob's ladder," or from this line from a familiar gospel song, "If Jesus goes with me, I'll go anywhere!" Even now as Bill looks back on his own struggles and hopes, his concerns and dreams as pastor of the Cote Brilliante Church family, much of his self-understanding and the shaping of his ministry can be traced to the influence of his pentecostal mother.

There were, of course, other touchstones that informed Bill's life and faith journey as a minister of the gospel of Jesus Christ. One of them was the black religious community of Knoxville and its oral tradition, which was a source of storytelling, wisdom sayings, and nurturing experiences. He recalls, for example, an interesting Afro-centric saying used by one of his early teachers, Brother W. E. Sims, who cautiously advised young people about the future: "The man who knows how will always have a job, but the one who knows why will always be his boss." In the context of his own life and faith pilgrimage, Bill Gillespie uses this saying to encourage people in his own community—young and old—to be all that they can be, to settle for nothing less than their best. Given the difficult and arduous struggle his inner-city church faces to respond to the needs of the voiceless poor, Pastor Gillespie finds himself involved daily with unwed mothers, high school dropouts, drug users, the disabled, and the semiskilled. "My ministry must be one of reaching out to these marginal people with a word from God which always spells "hope," not in what we say but what we be."

The more I dialogued with Pastor Gillespie, the clearer it became that the idea of "being" is at the center of his faith struggle and his under-standing of liberation in the black community. He believes, in his soul, that the church must somehow help the voiceless ones to climb Jacob's ladder by allowing them to settle for nothing less than what God intended them to be. "Can we not see that God intended a new being even for the voiceless ones in our midst? How can the church assist them in climbing Jacob's ladder?" Gillespie questioned. These are the haunting thoughts and deep questions that remain unresolved for Bill. Yet, in our conversa-tion about his struggle for clarity of faith and identity, he repeated a cryptic saying that still lingers in my own head and heart: "Be what you is, and not what you ain't. Because if you ain't what you is, you is what you ain't!"

I suspect to some extent, the whole of Bill's ministry and faith pilgrim-age is at least partially reflected in this folk saying. What it fully means for the poor and the voiceless in the black community, I am not sure. Yet, I also suspect that climbing Jacob's ladder might be easier if we would but ponder its deeper meaning. Invited, as we are, to a ministry of being, how can we best ponder the old Negro spiritual?

We are climbing Jacob's ladder
We are climbing Jacob's ladder
We are climbing Jacob's ladder
Soldiers of the Cross.

Every round goes higher, higher
Every round goes higher, higher

Every round goes higher, higher
Soldiers of the Cross.

Sinner, do you love my Jesus?
Sinner, do you love my Jesus?
Sinner, do you love my Jesus?
Soldiers of the Cross.

If you love Him, why not serve Him?
If you love Him, why not serve Him?
If you love Him, why not serve Him?
Soldiers of the Cross.

DISCUSSION NOTES

Even though Bill Gillespie grew up in the South in the 1930s, he seems, surprisingly, to have been untouched by racism—despite the generally hard times and the unrest of a nation caught up in modernization and racial polarization.

Bill's faith story and ministry reveal several interesting themes. An African-American minister, he finds his pastoral model in the biblical tradition of the eighth-century prophets rather than in examples set by modern-day successful and stoic church bureaucrats. The first theme, then, as revealed in this case, is the element of prophetic witness that informs his understanding of ministry in both the African-American community and his city, and that reinforces his feeling that the God of the Bible calls the church to be an agent of social change and the conscience of the wider society.

The second theme is criticism of unjust social structures that victimize people. In Bill's view of Christian faith, such structures are not only morally unjust but sinful in God's eyes. Real faith is not a "comfortable pew" that cushions middle-class Christians from the shock waves of a cruel world, but a "launching pad" for pursuit of God's justice and righteousness for the oppressed and suffering regardless of race.

The third theme is the clear ethical mandate to "feed the hungry and clothe the naked." Such an imperative is at the very heart of the way Bill reads the gospel of Jesus Christ. The fourth theme—"interracial good-will"—is often ignored or obscured in contemporary discussions of Christian ethics and liberation theology. Bill Gillespie's faith story makes the point for such generosity nicely.

Finally, the metaphor of Jacob's ladder is a rich symbol of hope and transformation to suffering people the world over. It should strike a universal chord in Christians regardless of race, color, class, sex, or moral persuasion. But despite its broad applicability, the particularity of the ladder image to the black experience in America is culturally significant. On the one hand, the metaphor of the ladder is tied in with an educational doctrine of progress and black achievement. On the other hand, the metaphor has a deeper religious implication of the way God summons the people, who are suffering under the yoke of oppression and domination, to greater faithfulness and authentic freedom. Thus, it may be useful in this case to think of "climbing Jacob's ladder" as a metaphor for both contagious faith and the embodiment of true liberation on the part of the morally sensitive person. The phrase, "We are climbing Jacob's ladder," evokes different responses in us all. We may wish to consider the following concerns and questions in Christian moral life.

Ethical Approach

1. How should the church respond to the stranger, the naked, and the poor in our communities?
2. What references in the Bible do you find to the poor?
3. Based on your view of the gospel of Jesus Christ, must the church stand in solidarity with the poor?

Issues for Reflection

1. What risks do you feel Pastor Gillespie took in his attempt to do ministry with marginal people?
2. Do churches in your community cooperate in providing assistance or programs that benefit the disadvantaged? If not, why not?
3. What insights or suggestions do you pick up from Pastor Gillespie's ministry that might be useful in your own life or vocation?

SUGGESTED READING

Genovese, Eugene D. *Roll, Jordan, Roll*. New York: Vintage Books, 1976.
Jones, William A., Jr. *God in the Ghetto*. Elgin, Ill.: Progressive Baptist Publishing House, 1979.
Kochman, Thomas. *Black and White: Styles in Conflict*. Chicago: University of Chicago Press, 1981.
Lincoln, C. Eric, ed. *The Black Experience in Religion*. New York: Doubleday, 1974.
Lubell, Samuel. *White and Black: Test of a Nation*. Harper & Row, 1964.
McCall, Emmanuel L. *Black Church Lifestyles*. Nashville: Broadman Press, 1986.
Plumpp, Sterling D. *Black Rituals*. Chicago: Third World Press, 1976.
Roberts, J. Deotis. *Roots of a Black Future: Family and Church*. Philadelphia: Westminster Press, 1980.

Thurman, Howard. *Deep River and the Negro Spiritual Speaks of Life and Death.* Richmond, Ind.: Friends United Press, 1975.

Wynn, Daniel W. *The Black Protest Movement.* New York: Philosophical Library, 1974.

12

SURVIVING
WITHOUT DIGNITY

"Being on welfare is an endless nightmare," said Samuel Lawford, a laid-off construction worker who lives in the foothills of southern Missouri. "As a man I'm accustomed to carrying my own weight and providing for my own family, but now all that has changed," muttered Samuel, as he put his arms around his oldest child. Like a frighteningly large number of Americans, Samuel has joined the ranks of the unemployed. As he talked about his plight, it was easy to feel his inner rage at the situation. As I looked into his eyes, I saw many emotions: fear, anger, powerlessness. Although Samuel came from a religious family, matters of church mission, faith in God, Christian service and charity had never figured high in his life. Sports and entertainment did, but prayer and contemplation did not. Church life was something that had seemed good and "respectable" for his wife and children, but not for Samuel himself. Religion and faith were largely outside his social world and self-understanding. His concern was to be a good provider and meet the needs of the family. That he did well for many years. Beyond family obligation, little seemed to matter until he was suddenly laid off. Then, embarrassed and wounded in spirit, Samuel Lawford was forced by the gravity of circumstances and his diminishing financial resources to leave his family so that they could receive welfare assistance.

Samuel is a thirty-two-year-old black male, married and the father of five. His wife, Betty, is a parttime secretary who works three days a week. Samuel and Betty have five beautiful children—Peter, 9, John, 7, Monika, 5, Gary, 4, and Alice Renae, 2. For the most part Samuel and Betty have a happy marriage, but unemployment has created tension and stress in the Lawford family. For one thing, Betty's dream of returning to school to improve her skills has changed. Marriage for ten years and the duties and problems of family life have also restricted her professional goals. "I don't want to throw my children out there in streets full of drugs, crime, violence . . ." she warned. "For that is what society expects from me. Besides, I care too much."

Before Samuel was laid off from his construction job, he was able to meet his monthly obligations and bills and provide for the basic economic and social needs of the family. With careful planning, on a combined monthly family income of approximately $1,400, he and Betty had been able to purchase a modest frame house, buy a used car, and provide the essentials for a growing family. Now, the financial reality of unemployment has drastically altered the emotional stability of the Lawford family. Shame has replaced pride. Conflict has ruptured family harmony. And poverty has threatened the moral fabric and spiritual bond of the faith. If one were to ask, "Are they surviving?" the immediate answer would be Yes but barely. And the real question would become, At what price?

Despite the pride he takes in his roles as father and husband, Samuel has been forced by a maze of bureaucratic regulations he does not fully understand to leave his home, his wife, and his family in order for them to receive assistance. For the most part, the family of seven receives a little over $375 a month in Aid to Families with Dependent Children (AFDC), and an additional $195 a month in food stamps. With this they survive, living day-to-day. But the main question before us, as people in human community is, Is this survival with dignity? Moreover, the issue is not what is being gained, but rather what is being lost. Can we see ourselves in the lives of Samuel and Betty? What social responsibility do we have, when we are confronted with a similar problem? I suspect that there are many people who can recognize the pain of a father forced to choose between "keeping the family together and going hungry" and allowing the family to be "kept" while he, the man of the house, is chased into exile. But, as one caseworker with the Division of Family Services bluntly acknowledged, "A wife is often financially better off with the husband not around the house!" But this situation created great emotional distress for Samuel Lawford. He has reached a point at which the misery and suffering engendered by his joblessness are almost unbearable.

Another issue people of faith must confront is poverty and its devastating effect on the lives of adults and children alike. For families like the Lawfords, welfare becomes a trap that locks opportunity out and misery in. As an unemployed person in exile, Samuel is on a road that leads nowhere. More often than not, fathers like Samuel Lawford are driven to roam the streets in strange cities, seeking whatever work they can find, sometimes forced to sleep in doorways, on benches in public parks, in overnight emergency shelters, in city jails, or in abandoned cars in order to survive. We have created a homeless person.

Left behind are children who never know the joy of a male presence in the home, and mothers who are without support and companionship. Sadly, economic statistics clearly show that mothers and children on welfare can barely make ends meet, that dependency and poverty are sustained, not eliminated, by the welfare system in this country, and that the greater danger of welfare may be the loss of self-esteem. It is also noteworthy that over half of all persons living in families headed by black women live in poverty. This is three times the poverty rate for families headed by a single male parent or a married couple.

"When you are out of work and black you do not know where to turn," lamented Samuel Lawford. The problem is even more acute in urban areas, where people seem not to care about an individual's struggles and life experiences. Black males are often tagged by society as "shiftless and lazy" in the workplace, and as "sexually careless and irresponsible" in the home. As for Samuel Lawford, the father of five children, this is how he characterized his own dilemma: "It seems that I get blamed as a negligent, no-good father because I left my family. But if I had stayed, the food supply would soon run out before the end of the month—and I was in no condition in my heart to see that happen. Either way, out of work I'm in a no-win situation.

Pausing momentarily, Samuel's voice grew stronger as he said, "Just look at me now, I'm only surviving day by day, step by step . . . Not much of a life, I dare say . . . Not much else except the hope of knowing that things can't get much worse—when you've got to look up to see the bottom. Away from my family as I am now, at least they're surviving; if I had stayed, they'd go hungry. Of course I still love my family, but I feel so angry, torn, and powerless . . . Where do I go from here?"

DISCUSSION NOTES

This case is not just about a man named Samuel who was forced by a job lay-off to put his family on welfare. Rather, at the core of this case is the tug of conscience and the human emotions of moral rage and pain. It is clear that Samuel and Betty Lawford are trapped in a cycle of powerlessness in the American social system. Based on data in the case, we find that Samuel and Betty feel a sense of dislocation and embarrassment over the pain and irony of their situation. They are angered; they are outraged that what they once had, as a family contributing to society, appears to be gradually slipping away amidst their hopelessness and Samuel's unemployment.

While the problem of unemployment is obviously important, I suspect that the wider issue for discussion is the precise meaning of "work" in our consumer culture, and its relationship to human dignity. For example, what value does our culture assign to work? What is the Christian understanding of work in relationship to human dignity? How is a person's worth to be measured when he or she is without an income-producing job for the family? Samuel's joblessness has strained his family life and threatened his manhood and his identity as the principal bread-winner for Betty and their five children.

Another issue that may claim our attention in this case is the cultural issue of racial stereotypes. Unfortunately, many people in our society depict the "welfare mothers" stereotypically—as being poor, lazy, and shiftless. Appropriately, we might ask, How can the ethically honest person in the Christian community unmask this pervasive stereotype? This important question deserves our serious attention and ethical reflection.

We may also raise the matter of the children as a focal point for discussion. Amidst the complex array of issues ranging from the meaning of work to racial stereotyping, it is easy to lose sight of the children as innocent victims. In our competitive society, children are often the real but silent victims of poverty and family disorganization. (Two resources that may be helpful for small group dialogue are *Black Families in White America* by Andrew Billingsley, and *Parenting for Peace and Justice* by Kathleen and James McGinnis.)

In the final analysis, other moral considerations that figure in the Lawford case include not only race and our ugly history of bigotry and discrimination—but also social class. Thus our own race and class shape the way we perceive the problems and the interpersonal dynamics between the silence of Samuel and Betty, on the one hand, and the cries of the children, on the other.

Ethical Approach

1. From your own point of view, what issues in the Lawford case claim your interest?

2. Is work essential for human dignity?
3. What is the biblical view of work and being a child of God?

Issues for Reflection

1. Should Samuel Lawford be forced to leave his wife and family for a "welfare handout"? Are there circumstances in which this sort of treatment would be acceptable?
2. What course of action seems appropriate in responding to the dilemmas and tensions in the Lawford family?
3. As a friend or Christian counselor, what steps would you take in dealing with Samuel's anger and rage?

SUGGESTED READING

Barnet, Richard J. *The Lean Years: Politics in the Age of Scarcity.* N.Y.: Simon & Schuster, 1980.

Christensen, Michael J. *City Streets, City People.* Nashville: Abingdon Press, 1988.

Ferrell, Frank, and Janet Ferrell. *Trevor's Place: The Story of the Boy Who Brings Hope to the Homeless.* San Francisco: Harper & Row, 1985.

Harrington, Michael. *The New American Poverty.* N.Y.: Holt, Rinehart & Winston, 1984.

Kochman, Thomas. *Black & White: Styles in Conflict.* Chicago: University of Chicago Press, 1981.

McNeil, Donald P., et al. *Compassion: A Reflection on the Christian Life.* Garden City, N.Y.: Doubleday, 1982.

Nelson, Jack A. *Hunger for Justice.* Maryknoll, N.Y.: Orbis Books, 1980.

Nouwen, Henri. *Making All Things New.* San Francisco: Harper & Row, 1981.

Sider, Ronald J., ed. *Lifestyle in the Eighties.* Philadelphia: Westminster Press, 1988.

Stivers, Robert L., et al. *Christian Ethics: A Case Method Approach.* Maryknoll, N.Y.: Orbis Books, 1989.

West, Cornel. *Prophecy Deliverance!* Philadelphia: Westminster Press, 1982.

CASE
13

A BOY AND HIS
SUPERMARKET CART

"Now let me get this right," said the counselor. "You have a makeshift supermarket cart that you use to steal automobile parts in order to help feed your brothers and sisters?" "Yes, that's right," Kirk replied, as he held his tear-streaked face in his hands. The counselor, Father Botkins, is a priest and ten-year family friend. The Lincoln Housing Complex, one of the roughest urban slums in St. Louis is in the neighborhood in which he has served.

There is a sociological school of thought that sees any society—religious or secular—as composed of two groups: an *in*-group and an *out*-group. The *in*-group may be characterized as the norm-setters, the decision-makers, and the power-brokers of a given community, those who have the muscle to create cohesiveness and achieve a purpose. Conversely, the *out*-group may be marked by powerlessness, poverty, and family disintegration. Reflective of the acceptance of this conceptual framework, I suspect that most of the folks of the Lincoln Housing Complex saw themselves as virtually powerless and condemned to the life of the *out*-group. Casual observation suggests that at least the power-brokers and *in*-group leaders saw the Lincoln neighborhood that way: a place where the brutal scars of despair drown out the echoes of hope!

Kirk Jenkins is sixteen. He is not a member of St. Mark's Church, but he has attended its day school since he was seven. Kirk is the second of eight children born to his attractive mother, Margaret Jenkins. Margaret is a single parent. She is in her late thirties and a very hardworking and caring parent, who spent most of her teenage years in the Mississippi Delta in the deep South. She came to St. Louis in the mid-1960s. Margaret has held a variety of low-paying jobs, including "soul food" caterer, parttime secretary, clerk, and domestic worker for a family in Ladue, Missouri, a wealthy suburb of St. Louis. Although she has been engaged to be married three times in the last six years, marriage always seems out of her grasp.

The neighborhood in which the Jenkins family lives has not helped their problem either. It is a rough section of the city, with all of the problems of urban life: gang warfare, crime, high unemployment, overcrowding, drug abuse, rape, prostitution, child molestation. Kirk, his mother, and the rest of the children live in a small, rundown apartment. Their rent is more than one-third of their monthly income.

Their limited income, Kirk complained to Father Botkins, means, "We barely have enough to get by, because all of our money is spent on surviving." His voice grew stronger, as Kirk continued, "When you gotta survive, you find a way or you make one!" "What do you mean by that?" retorted Father Botkins. "I mean you take your chances to help the family however you can." "Even if it means stealing?" A long pause followed the priest's question, and Kirk reluctantly whispered, "Well, I don't know." Father Botkins gently responded, "You don't know what?" "You know, the matter of stealing being always wrong. That's the reason I came to you," Kirk answered. "My friends think it shouldn't bother me so much, and even my mother don't know where I'm getting the extra money from. But she's starting to suspect something. I feel bad. What should I do?"

But, without giving the priest a chance to speak, Kirk shouted, "Please don't preach to me, 'Thou shalt not steal'! In these streets, Father, you learn how to survive, how to look out for yourself—even if it means ripping off a few hubcaps." Father Botkins didn't say a word. He knew well the unwritten laws of ghetto life. So many people who live impoverished in the city slums they call home have come from rural communities where things were tough. But here, in this "dark pit," as they call it, they have *nothing*. "Nothing" is *all* they have. Rootless and jobless, many of the urban dwellers are condemned to a squatter's existence. Kirk and his brothers and sisters, for whom he scraped together pennies, were no exception to the rule of victimization and the seemingly endless life of poverty.

With his hand gently resting on Kirk's shoulder, Father Botkins said, "Well, Kirk, what do you want me to do?" "I want to stop this mess of stealing, but I don't know if I can. It makes me feel bad and crazy," responded the young man. The tension in his voice was conspicuous. "Everyone has problems coping. Anyway, just because you're young and sitting here in my office doesn't mean you're either bad or crazy," said Father Botkins. "Tell me, how did you get started stealing?" Kirk's tense expression broke as he began to speak. "Well, I started in the streets when I was six, making a few bucks with my supermarket cart. Then I was just collecting junk, scraps of chrome from old cars. Later on, I did errands for junkies and drug pushers—but I never touched the stuff myself, though . . . Man, all of my friends were doing somethin' to make a few bucks." His body shifted in the chair as he continued in a soft voice. "We all were taught that if you don't do somethin' and get somethin', you never have nothin', not even respect." "I see," said Father Botkins casually. "Then what?"

"Well, things were going good at first and we were real honest, using our carts for scraps. Suddenly, my little sister got low sick, and we didn't have insurance. Our family needed extra money for her. We just seemed to be going down deeper in a hole." "How do you mean?" inquired Father Botkins. "Can you imagine living in that dirty pit we call home for nearly all of your life? I figured that a little stealing with my cart wouldn't only help out, it would be a way up in society. Strange, isn't it?" His voice trailed off. "I started taking from Mr. Conroy's used car lot at night and taking the stuff to other places for extra money." He paused and then blurted out, "Was that so wrong, Father Botkins? You have no idea what a hellhole this place is, and we want out! Seriously!"

"I do know Kirk, I've been doing the Lord's work here for ten years. And I think you should quit this stealing business before you get hurt or caught by the law." A long silence followed before Kirk replied. "Maybe eventually, I'll feel ashamed or embarrassed."

"Does your mother know about this?" asked Father Botkins. "Oh no! If she found out, she'd kill me. My mother would be a nervous wreck— she'd fall to pieces over this. Father Botkins, promise me you won't tell her. You know my young sisters and brothers look up to me." "I won't tell, if you promise me you will stop stealing . . . God knows I do care deeply about you and the welfare of your whole family." The priest's voice rose and he seemed almost to be shouting. "Frankly, I'm waiting for your response!" Replied Kirk defensively, "Well, I just don't know if I can promise. Nearly everyone has some kind of a problem. This is mine." "Before you spoke of 'we' and 'us,' but now you say 'me' and 'mine.' You can't dismiss the problem just like that," exclaimed Father Botkins. "A lot is at stake. Do you hear me?"

Kirk was now sitting on the edge of his chair staring wide-eyed at the crucifix on the wall, "Just exactly what am I to do?" he asked. "Stop,

stop the stealing!'' "No, no!" cried Kirk quickly. "It ain't that easy!" "Do you have faith in yourself?'' "What does faith have to do with survival? With our survival as a family?'' It was as if Father Botkins were held strangely captive, helplessly thrown off guard by Kirk's question. He seemed to search, reaching deep inside himself for something to break the tension of the moment. Then he said quietly, "Faith may have everything to do with it—faith to change and go in another direction.''

"Come on, be realistic, Father.'' "Faith is realistic,'' the priest quickly retorted. "It takes more faith to face your problems and change than to accept what happens and let yourself be flushed down the toilet.'' "Sure, you can say that as a minister, judging other people and all,'' responded Kirk. Father Botkins reassured him. "It's all right, I'm not judging you. I'm concerned with what you do with your life.'' Citing a verse from Psalms he continued, "The Lord upholds all who are falling, and raises up all who are bowed down.''

Nervously, Kirk said, "There you go preaching to me again! People who live here don't need preaching at. We make our daily bread the best way we can—collecting things and getting things from the trash dumps and selling them. Why do I have to tell you? You know the stuff we put up with living in this hole. People here live off the trash they breathe.'' "Yes Kirk," said Father Botkins. "We've been through all of that, but why do you have to steal? I know that the struggle for survival is very hard in this neighborhood—the constant scraping for food, shelter, and clothing wears all of us down sometimes. But have faith in yourself. Are we not stooping as low as trash when we take what another person earned?''

Kirk stormed out of Father Botkins's office, both anger and shame on his face. The next morning, Father Botkins caught a glimpse of Kirk from a distance in the parking lot of the neighborhood supermarket. He pressed his way through a small crowd to see Kirk. "Why did you leave my office so suddenly?'' he asked. "I was tired and restless and had to go,'' said Kirk. "A lot of what you said in the office jolted me, especially the stuff about self-belief and faith, and facing up to your own problems. Sometimes I feel unwanted and insecure, even though I know my mother loves me. With all the other kids, there's hardly enough love and time to go around.'' Kirk stood gazing at the flood of people at the supermarket. "It may sound silly and strange, but I often feel more secure when I'm out roaming with my old cart than when I'm with my family.''

The opportunity was now there for Father Botkins to come back to Kirk's real problem and the matter of faith and self-belief. As a Christian minister, he wanted desperately to say more about the gift of faith, and "faith's way of sharing God's love and concern for us in Jesus Christ." Remembering their previous conversation, the last thing he wanted was to give Kirk a mini-sermon on "the virtues of faith and the vices of stealing." He knew that would be morally disastrous. As Father Botkins reasoned, "That approach would strip Kirk of whatever threads of dignity or self-respect he had left!"

Instead, Father Botkins firmly said, "Let's go over to your house and talk some more." Before Kirk could respond, there was a noise in the parking lot, and people rapidly left. Kirk and Father Botkins heard the siren of a police car. Kirk's heartbeat increased as the piercing sound drew near. He realized that two of his close friends had just been arrested for shoplifting. Trying hard to keep his composure, Kirk was visibly pained and frightened. He wondered, "Am I any better than them? Will I be next?"

But unknown to Kirk, Father Botkins had told his mother about Kirk's problem and the supermarket cart after Kirk had stormed out of his office. Now, puzzled and arguing with his conscience, Father Botkins wondered, Did I do the right thing? Does Margaret have the right to know? What is the faithful and caring thing to do? When should a confidence be broken?

DISCUSSION NOTES

Is stealing always wrong? is the sort of moral question that has baffled Christian counselors, social ethicists, and other concerned persons for many generations. This case emerges out of a counseling situation involving Kirk Jenkins, a sixteen-year-old inner-city black youth of North St. Louis. While the issue of whether stealing is ever morally justifiable is the obvious issue of the case, also at issue are the matters of self-esteem and the social dangers of growing up poor in dark ghettos. Kirk Jenkins, however, does not fit the classic American stereotype of the ruthless, shiftless, and socially aggressive black youth. While doing what is necessary to survive on the streets of an urban jungle, Kirk is not without conscience and passionate concern for the welfare of his mother, Margaret, and his siblings.

The reader of this case will observe Kirk's debate of conscience and the contemplative spirit evident in his relationship with Father Botkins, a Catholic priest and longtime friend of the family. I suspect that the issue of poverty in urban America is never really easy for Christians to discuss.

It tends to give most middle-class Christians, black and white, a case of "ethical heartburn" and guilt. Perhaps one reason for such attitudes and reactions on our part is our moral awareness that behind the statistics of poverty are "human faces" like Kirk's, Margaret's, and Father Botkins'. Each one cares. Each one is torn and seared by the ravages of poverty. Indeed, Father Botkins, as counselor, agonized over what it means for children and struggling parents to be condemned to live in the "dirty pit" of poverty. Sadly, the case reveals, to some degree, that for too many poverty reaps a harvest of shame in the ghetto.

Regular group discussion may also revolve around the theological issue and the dialectic between faith and survival. Kirk Jenkins appears to be ethically troubled about his stealing, but even more perplexed as to whether faith in God can make a difference in his future behavior. What moral directions or nurturing would you offer to Kirk?

Ethical Approach

1. How can God's call to love, oneness, and compassion be mirrored in the lives of ghetto children?
2. What is the task of clergy or laity in providing guidance for teen-agers?
3. What is the faithful and caring thing to do?

Issues for Reflection

1. What are the moral dilemmas of stealing in the interest of survival?
2. Is it hypocritical for Father Botkins to ask Kirk to stop stealing without suggesting any real alternative, such as parttime employment around the parish?
3. How do you assess the role of Kirk's mother, a single parent?

SUGGESTED READING

Butcher, M. J. *The Negro in American Culture.* 2d ed. New York: Alfred A. Knopf, 1972.

David, Jay, ed. *Growing Up Black.* New York: William Morrow & Co., 1968.

Ewald, William R., Jr., ed. *Environment and Public Policy: The Next Fifty Years.* Bloomington: Indiana University Press, 1968.

Franklin, John H., ed. *Color and Race.* Boston: Beacon Press, 1968.

Gardner, Howard. *Frames of Mind: The Theory of Multiple Intelligences.* New York: Basic Books, 1983.

Harrison-Ross, Phyllis, and B. Wyden. *The Black Child: A Parents' Guide.* New York: Peter H. Wyden, 1973.

Herber, Lewis. *Crisis in Our Cities*. Englewood Cliffs, N.J.: Prentice-Hall, 1965.

Kramer, P., and F. L. Holborn, eds. *The City in American Life*. New York: G. P. Putnam's Sons, 1970.

Levy, Gerald E. *Ghetto School*. New York: Western Publishing, 1970.

Newman, Oscar. *Park-Mall Lawndale: St. Louis Urban Renewal Design Center*. St. Louis: Washington University, 1968.

Rogers, Donald B., ed. *Urban Church Education*. Birmingham, Ala.: Religious Education Press, 1964.

Rudwick, E. M. *Race Riot at East St. Louis*. Carbondale, Ill.: Southern Illinois University Press, 1964.

Waskow, Arthur I. *From Race Riot to Sit-In—1919 and the 1960s*. New York: Doubleday & Co., 1966.

Wren, Brian. *Education for Justice*. Maryknoll, N.Y.: Orbis Books, 1977.

CASE

14

RESPECT YOURSELF,
RESPECT WOMEN!

"Back then we didn't have much except pride and the Prayer House . . . We were poor and mama would diligently drag us out of bed at 3:30 in the morning for a quick breakfast, just before the bus arrived around four o'clock to pick us up for the cotton fields," exclaimed Clarence Powell in a tone of moral concern about the way things were in a small Southern town of the mid-1950s. Meet the main character of this case study, Clarence Powell, age fifty, and reflect with me upon his faith pilgrimage and struggles, hewed in part out of the social fabric of a life familiar to many blacks in the South.

Clarence is a tall, loose-limbed man, with a stoic, bronze face, hair verging on jet black, a firm chin, and honest brown eyes. His brisk walk and lean frame help identify him as a man of genuine sobriety. Warm and friendly, Clarence hails from Earle, Arkansas, a predominantly black town where "cotton is king." In this largely agricultural community located in the northeastern part of the state, the drama of his early life unfolded. In the 1950s, the economic lifeblood of this small town of 2300 people was the booming cotton industry. Even today, a visitor traveling through this region is struck by two contrasting realities: the rich black soil that nurtured the lucrative cotton industry, which was largely run by whites who owned the land and controlled the capital, and the black tenants who worked the land and lived in squatter-dwellings or shacks that dotted the countryside.

In Earle, the common laborers who daily worked the fields often would joke among themselves—far from the ears of white landowners—about life in the fields: "Where cotton is king, the bucket got a hole in it for de colored folks!" The world into which Clarence was born nurtured a neocolonial lifestyle, in which Southern whites were largely "well-off," or the privileged class, and blacks were viewed as "less-than," or the disprivileged class. This disprivileged class was made up of the rural poor—black and white, the common laborers, the field hands, and the tenant farmers who wholeheartedly gave themselves to the land but did not reap a fair return on their labor. Clarence's childhood world perpetuated a view of people that is reflected in this saying: "If you are white, you're all right; if you are brown, stick around; but if you are black, get back!" And blacks in the 1950s were literally "back": they rode in the *back* of the bus; they prepared food *back* in the kitchen; they ate in *back* sections of public restaurants marked "colored"; they slept in *back* seats of cars while visiting relatives or friends; and they worked long hours *back* in the cotton fields to produce things they could not afford to consume, while consuming things they did not produce. Perhaps the real irony of Clarence's childhood—in which dreams were easily deferred and hopes were at the mercy of a segregated society—was that he did grow up. He did survive. He persevered. He fought the odds. He ran against the wind. He struggled to overcome. For good or for ill, he learned well the painful lessons of Southern history in his own Crittenden County: without black struggle there can be no progress.

By his own story, the fruits of progress did not come easily or without faith in God and the fervent prayers of his mother, who was affectionately known in Earle as "L.A." Recalling his difficult days as a young laborer in the cotton fields, Clarence spoke about his mother and her faith: "To my surprise, mama would often wake up in the wee hours of the morning, around two or three, just praying so hard for all of the children—that the Lord God would allow no hurt, harm, or danger to befall any of us while we were working in the blazing heat, chopping cotton from sunup to sundown for only a dollar a day . . . Sometimes the cotton choppers would jokingly shout, 'Another day, another dollar!' . . . But in truth, we only made seventy-five cents a day when you consider twenty-five cents went for a daily sack lunch—usually a small can of pork 'n beans, crackers, and a Baby Ruth candy bar . . . that was it. But that didn't matter much; mama still prayed harder for us that God would somehow make things a little better . . . Although mama is dead now, I still hear her prayers sometimes, ringing in my head. It's funny as I look back; she thought that none of us were awake that early in the morning—since she believed that each Christian should pray in secret . . . But I, for one, heard her secret prayers often."

The interview for this case study took place in Clarence's home in

Chicago. How he got from Earle, Arkansas, to Chicago is also a lesson in social irony, but it is a different piece of his wider story of struggle and faith as an African-American. As we spoke, Clarence slowly relaxed and began to share more of the hurts and hopes of his mother and the shaping experiences of his youth. I asked, "What was your mother like? How did she impact you as a young man?"

"As I said, times were hard, but life still had to go on, being that we all were in the same boat . . . merely scraping to just make a penny. The name of the game was survival then; everybody who could work usually made a day in the fields, one way or another. We were all young and full of energy . . . As I think about it, my mother gave me a positive outlook on life; and what faith or self-confidence I have really came from her. What I remember most about mama was her moaning and low-key singing around the house—such things as, 'Lord Jesus, I pray Thee, please bestow on me a heart of thanksgiving. Please, dear God, take care of my children and my neighbors . . . I pray Thee in Thy tender mercy, to watch over my little boy Clarence' . . . For some reason, mama seemed to favor me a lot; we had a special relationship that I can't really explain."

In this small family, from which his father was constantly absent, the bonds of love and mutual respect were exceedingly strong between him and his mother. But he sadly confided, "I didn't really know my father that well—and what I did know about him deeply hurt me . . . My mother was the dominant role model for me." It was difficult for L.A. to raise her black family, especially in the South in the 1950s. She functioned essentially as a "single parent" and did it all because Clarence's father was seldom around. "If it had not been for God and mama's loving, hardworking spirit," confessed Clarence, "I don't know what exactly would have become of us . . . She was a fighter and never gave up!"

While it was apparent that L.A.'s faith may not have been outwardly displayed in public worship, it did affect young Clarence as he struggled with issues of survival and self-esteem in a world not of his own making. Personal testimony to one's faith is often partial to irony and surprise. One of the ironies of Clarence's childhood is that the lack of a positive father image, apparently, did not distort his self-image or destroy his self-confidence.

Clarence graduated from Dunbar High School, with honors, in 1954. With the encouragement and prayers of his mother, Clarence wrote the lyrics for the school's song, "Dear Old Dunbar." Clarence's song is still the school song today, more than thirty years later, and is sung with pride as old classmates gather periodically for reunion and fellowship.

After his graduation from high school, Clarence Powell joined the Army. For many blacks, the armed forces represented a move up, away from, and out of the blazing heat of the Southern cotton fields. (Hand picking wages at that time for the laborer in Crittenden County ranged from $2.50 to $3.00 for every 100 pounds of cotton picked. Clarence became known as a fast-cotton-picker because he and his mother could literally pick a bail of cotton per day!) After his tour of duty in the armed service, Clarence enrolled, on the G.I. Bill, into an electronics technical school in Chicago and completed the course of study. He also did further professional study at Chicago's Kennedy-King College. He now holds a position with the U.S. Postal Service, where he has worked for more than twenty years. The lifestyle of the Powell family is solidly middle class and reflects the trappings of an American success story. They own a comfortable home in the suburbs of Chicago; Joetta, Clarence's wife, is employed fulltime with a large company in the downtown Loop; Gregory, their son, is a graduate student at Columbia University's school of journalism; and Elaine, their daughter, an accomplished pianist, holds the position of minister of music at her local church on the South Side.

If, indeed, it is true that the lessons of hard times often nurture character, then growing up in the South was a blessing in disguise for Clarence Powell. Despite the external forces of racial discrimination that often made for death, L.A.'s robust faith apparently made for life, which was victorious over the chilling powers of death. Clarence's voice grew increasingly joyful as he spoke of his mother and his youth. "Because of my mother's faith in God and confidence in me, I always felt that I could make it and get a good job."

Then Clarence told me a family story, something that occurred when he was twelve and shows how his mother demonstrated her own faith in a trying situation: In the cold of winter their house burned to the ground, and members of the family were forced to find temporary shelter with relatives and friends. With no property insurance, they needed help badly. Virtually penniless, L.A. had no alternative but to seek a loan from a local bank in Earle. According to Clarence, she boldly walked into the bank on a cold, rainy day and asked the white receptionist to set up a meeting for her with the president, Mr. Nisbet. "Lady, did I hear you right?" asked the receptionist in an arrogant tone, that seemed to question L.A.'s human dignity. "We don't allow niggers here to see or speak to the bank president!" "But I said I wish to speak to the president," L.A. asserted, in a strong, crisp voice. Before long everyone in the bank could hear the two women quarreling, including Mr. Nisbet. He emerged from his office in the back of the bank to find out about the commotion and to settle the dispute. To the surprise of many, he ended up giving this persistent and stubborn black woman a hearing. And she convinced him to approve a loan for the rebuilding of her house. "I saw my mama doing these sorts of things growing up," averred Clarence, "and maybe this is the reason I feel so strongly that black men today need to respect women and respect themselves . . . Mama's faith, as I think about it, taught me faith in myself and *respect* for others."

Perhaps what most disturbs Clarence Powell is the issue of respect for women in the black community. He feels that the majority of black men in America have little or no respect for their own women. "They often leave them [women] out in the cold to fend for themselves with small children and limited skills, while the men are about doing other things." Crucial to his own faith story is his conviction that churches and communities must take action about the lack of respect for women, especially marginal women who are forced to live on welfare or not live at all. As a man of faith, Clarence is disturbed and worried that we are gradually removing hope from the lives of our young people by allowing them to just "walk-over" their mothers as if those mothers were doormats.

Toward the end of the interview, I posed the question, "If this is a problem for people of faith in our own community, what do we do about it?" Pausing to muse on the question, Clarence gazed at a ray of light beaming through the basement window and replied, "I don't know a whole lot about the Bible and how it views women, although I'm a lay officer in my local church; but I do know that Christian faith upholds respect for the beauty of womanhood . . . I strongly insist, for instance, that Gregory respect his mother—always; he knows that I'll knock his block off about this! But this element of respect for women seems to be gravely missing in our own community today, and what we should do about it I can't say exactly . . . All I know is that my mother would tan my hide if I got out of line. Maybe we need to go back to scripture on this problem . . ."

DISCUSSION NOTES

This case is about the faith pilgrimage and moral struggles of Clarence Powell, an African-American Christian, whose life story and character have been shaped in part by the social forces of segregation in the old South. For nearly every black child of Clarence's day—the early 1950s—suffering and moral struggle were the price to be paid for progress. The theme of perseverance is expressed well in the saying, "Without struggle there can be no progress."

The important principles and values of self-esteem, prayer, and hard work are inherent in the religious life and culture of black people in America. And the principles of community—sharing, respecting, caring, praying, and empowering—are the connecting links of the life stories of black people as they seek to understand Christian faith, scripture, and cultural tradition. For African-American Christians such as Clarence, this case may be used to highlight the value of "respect" and the importance of building a sense of community. Hence, we may ponder these religio-ethical questions: What is respect? How is it imaged in this case? What is community? How is it mirrored in the faith pilgrimage and life story of Clarence Powell?

In small group discussion, you may want to grapple with the meaning of "respect" as it is evidenced in the particularities and progression in Clarence's life story. I find the word "respect" very interesting and analytically compelling in terms of a relational study. Dictionaries agree that a number of words connote *respect*. These include "worth," "esteem," "honor," "equal regard," "privacy," "intimacy," and "selfhood." In regular group discussion, these may be used by pastors and teachers as guide words and signs of hope to ameliorate the social condition in our time. As persons of conscience and faith, we are challenged today as never before to consider the essential ingredients or motifs necessary for the development of a viable ethic of respect—beginning, undoubtedly, in the family, the church, and the broader community of humankind. It seems to me that we have an obligation not only to do those things in human community that enhance the value and meaning of respect, but also to see respect, ultimately, as a gift of God.

The central theme of this case is emphatically clear: *Respect yourself!* As a man of faith, Clarence insists on respect as a pivotal shaping value in his own family. In short, respect is the right stuff for whatever reason and in all seasons of moral development, from youth to old age. At the practical level of community life, we may wish to consider and ponder what the writer of Proverbs had to say about the central theme of respect:

My son, do not forget my teaching,
    but let your heart keep my commandments;
for length of days and years of life
    and abundant welfare will they give you.
Let not loyalty and faithfulness forsake you;
    bind them about your neck,

write them on the tablet of your heart.

. . . .

Trust in the Lord with all your heart,
and do not rely on your own insight.
(Prov. 3:1–3, 5)

Ethical Approach

1. What is the responsibility of the church regarding the plight of the single parent?
2. Is there a moral link between the biblical imperatives "Honor thy father and mother" and "Set the oppressed free"?
3. What levels of moral thinking may enhance or increase respect for women and other persons in your own family and community?

Issues For Reflection

1. What comparisons, if any, can be drawn between Clarence's formative experiences and your own story of faith and struggle?
2. In your view, what progress has been made in black-white relations today?
3. From the perspective of Christian faith, what sort of racial barriers must be overcome in American society in the 1990s?

SUGGESTED READING

Chapman, Abraham, ed. *Black Voices: An Anthology of Afro-American Literature*. New York: Mentor Books, 1968.

Cone, James H. *For My People: Black Theology and the Black Church*. Maryknoll, N.Y.: Orbis Books, 1984.

Grant, Jacquelyn. "Black Theology and the Black Women." In *Black Theology: A Documentary History 1966–1979*, edited by Gayraud S. Wilmore and James H. Cone. Maryknoll, N.Y.: Orbis Books, 1979.

Harding, Vincent. *There Is a River*. New York: Harcourt Brace Jovanovich, 1981.

Hughes, Langston. *Laughing to Keep from Crying*. New York: Henry Holt, 1952.

King, Charles H., Jr. *Fire in My Bones*. Grand Rapids: Wm. B. Eerdmans, 1983.

Kochman, Thomas. *Black and White: Styles in Conflict*. Chicago: University of Chicago Press, 1981.

Lincoln, C. Eric. *The Black Church and the African American Experience*. Durham, N.C.: Duke University Press, 1990.

Plumpp, Sterling D. *Black Rituals*. Chicago: Third World Press, 1972.

Redding, J. Saunders. *The Lonesome Road: The Story of the Negro's Part in America*. Garden City, N.Y.: Doubleday & Co., 1958.

Sterling, Dorothy, ed. *Speak Out in Thunder Tones*. New York: Doubleday & Co., 1973.

————— ed. *The Trouble They Seen*. New York: Doubleday & Co., 1976.

Walker, Alice. "In Search of Our Mothers' Gardens." In *Black Theology: A Documentary History, 1966–1979*, edited by Gayraud S. Wilmore and James H. Cone. Maryknoll, N.Y.: Orbis Books, 1979.

CASE

15

TURN A NEGATIVE POSITIVE

"I can still hear her words now, echoing in my ears," exclaimed Ronald, "that an idle mind is the devil's workshop." As a people of faith and moral struggle, African-Americans have a fair share of "dos and don'ts" and certain standards of social behavior and conduct in the home, church, and the institutions of the black community. Understanding those moral rules and religious principles is important for better understanding human nature and society.

Ronald Packnett's life story and faith pilgrimage are not extraordinarily different from those of many of his contemporaries who grew up on the South Side of Chicago in the early 1960s. "Our house was always filled to the brim with loads of uncles, aunts, cousins, nephews and nieces—who added plenty of laughter and tension to our family and to life with my fifteen brothers and sisters. We grew up knowing about the negatives of the ghetto but somehow found ways not to get trapped by all the craziness and madness on the streets," explained Ronald as he shared with me his own faith story.

Ronald Packnett is thirty-seven years old. An ordained Baptist minister and graduate of Yale Divinity School, he is currently pastoring the Central Avenue Baptist Church in St. Louis, Missouri, a congregation with more than 400 members. Ronald was born to Nicholas Broadnax and Brittany Noel, both of Chicago. His mother was a dedicated Christian who strongly believed that everything that happens to a person in life, good or bad, is the will of God. Sensitive to the important role of religion in life, she firmly believed, and instructed her children, that success in work or play stems from the ability to see God in everything. She often warned the children, for example, never to arrogantly state their life or career goals without first reverently saying, "If the Lord willing, I'll do this or that . . ." In his mother's religious philosophy and language, the dominant reality was that God must be first in our lives. The phrase "if the Lord willing" was a kind of daily ritual that ran like the main thread in a spider web and united the whole fabric of life for this struggling family. The phrase was also a way of keeping in check what Ronald Packnett calls "our sinful nature," which could easily get a young person in trouble— especially one not familiar with street culture on Chicago's South Side. So, the religious language used to talk about personal goals and challenges made a big difference in the Packnett family. For the family as a whole, God-speech was a part of everything.

Ronald's grandmother also played a crucial role in shaping his character and faith pilgrimage. Grandma Ella, as she was called, was a product of Southern tradition in the pre-civil rights period. Raised in the small town of Centerville, Mississippi, near the Louisiana border, her spiritual roots were grounded in the fabric of Southern black community life. During the hot summer months, Ronald and his cousins would journey by train from Chicago to Centerville, where they would participate in the annual family ritual of working the fields, going to church, and playing on the farm. Grandma Ella owned two hundred acres of rich farmland, on which the Packnett family grew cotton, watermelons, beans, and other vegetables for the family.

While visiting for the summer, the children were always reminded of three rules of conduct laid down by Grandma Ella. Rule one was respect for the local customs and manners of the white community of Centerville. At the practical level of social discourse, this required, for instance, that blacks should always speak to whites politely, saying, "Yes, sir" or "No, sir." "That way," Grandma Ella advised, "you won't get yourselves hurt or aggravate the rednecks of the devil's workshop . . . Remember this, children, so long as you're here in Mississippi." For Ronald, this strange Southern custom not only offended his moral sensibilities and made him angry but required enormous self-discipline of both the heart and tongue to abide by. He occasionally rebelled against this pattern of Southern behavior but quickly discovered that it was not in his best interest to be regarded as an "uppity" or "sassety" black youth. Ronald recalled, for example, an incident involving one of his high-spirited cousins from Chicago. In less than a week, cousin Joseph was speedily put on a midnight train and sent back to Chicago, after he jokingly stuck out his tongue at a little white girl in Centerville. "Grandma Ella knew instinctively that sort of nonsensical gesture could cause a young black child to lose his life," said Ronald.

Ironically, it was from this negative climate of social restraint in the South that Ronald came to better appreciate the value of discipline and toughness in his struggle for dignity and freedom as a child of God. For Ronald, toughness of spirit and hard work reflected Grandma Ella's stern words that, "An idle mind is the devil's workshop." As Grandma saw it, if cousin Joseph had been busy with his assigned chores on the farm, he wouldn't have had idle time for practical jokes. The real challenge facing Ronald was the struggle to turn a negative experience into a positive one.

The second moral value upon which Grandma Ella insisted was the importance of the church, "the house of God," as the community elders would say. " 'Young folks today won't get nowhere with their lives in this world, unless they respect the house of God first,' she would say," explained Ronald. As he remembered it, the small community of Centerville was the kind of place that faithfully gathered—especially around the church. It was at the church that the Packnett family would gather for worship, praise, and mutual encouragement. The church was the center of social life for sisters and brothers, parents and grandparents, uncles and aunts, friends and relatives. For the black community, the church was the hub that held things together. It is interesting to note that this was especially true regarding the way young people were raised and disciplined in the Packnett family. I suspect that many of the traditional moral values held in high regard by the family were often reinforced by the church. Grandma Ella laid down the "law," and this so-called law was epitomized in such sayings as, "A hard head makes a soft butt!" and "Spare the rod, spoil the child." Such sayings apparently enabled Ronald and his siblings to better cope with the trials of being black in the American South in the early 1960s.

A third moral value that Grandma Ella impressed upon Ronald was self-determination and productivity. "America is a land of opportunity only for those who make opportunity happen," quipped Ronald, remembering her words. Centerville was noted for its high cotton production. And perhaps it was in this climate of toil and work that the value of self-determination took hold in the young man's life.

The long summers spent in the South were joyful but troublesome for Ronald because of Grandma Ella's insistence that all the folks in her household attend church each Sunday. Stern, even puritanical in religious matters, she required that young Ronald pay close attention to the fire and brimstone sermons that thundered above his head as they patiently sat in the old, country Baptist church on the edge of town. Certain teenage social activities—drinking, dancing, smoking, and playing cards—were strictly prohibited in the Packnett family. But more than "off limits" socially, they were considered to be works of the devil!

Particularly troublesome for Ronald was his relationship with his father, Nicholas Broadnax. To his regret, the two were never close. Ronald described them as having "a sort of love-hate affair," because his father was more invisible than visible, especially as a positive moral force in the home. His mother, Brittany Noel, however, filled the void, and her religious beliefs seem to have greatly influenced his character development and the direction his life took in Christian ministry.

At sixteen, Ronald faced a critical turning point in his life: the sudden death of his father. Ronald suspects that his father's sudden death was somehow related to his drinking problem. In any event, this was obviously a painful experience for the entire family. Ronald vividly remembers that on the night before the funeral he prayed hard to God on behalf of his father's soul. Reflecting on that sad evening, he laments, "I prayed all night to God for my father's soul and well-being . . . I prayed that since he was not such a good Christian man on earth, maybe, just maybe in heaven he would be different; I prayed that I could have the relationship *in heaven*, that I never had with him on earth—as a son to a father. Those were difficult times for me and the family." He further explained, "In the whole thing of the love-hate relationship with my father, there is still some tension and anger inside of me when I think about my own inability to reconcile who my father was . . . And I really did love him, despite what he did to himself that affected all the rest of us in the family." The distancing and the pain he experienced in this father-son relationship were responsible for Ronald Packnett's adult spiritual growth. As pastor of an inner-city Baptist church in St. Louis, he brings skill and sensitivity to complex issues of ministry and pastoral counseling specifically because of his inner struggles.

It would appear that Ronald Packnett's understanding of faith and its role in our fragmented lives prompts him to see a God who is not judgmental but merciful, compassionate, and steadfast in love toward us. Ronald says that because of his struggle with his father and the strict moral urgings of his Grandma Ella, "a burden of suffering hangs over my soul." But then he clarified his faith, saying, "The God of the black church has always met black people, individually and collectively, in their deep valleys of suffering, pointing them to the mountaintop of hope, . . . though we can't fully understand God's way."

When discussing God's relationship to the continuing suffering of African-Americans, Packnett simply affirms, in the familiar words of the old black spiritual, that we "will understand it better by and by." "God allows certain things to happen to us to make us stronger as Christians," exclaimed Ronald. For him, faith in the God who "sides with the oppressed" is a great mystery of the church and a mystery for those who try and follow the basic moral and social teachings of Jesus Christ. In his theological view, what the church of Jesus Christ can do is proclaim the power of the mystery of how God comes to us in our moments of suffering and travail. This insight of faith was particularly acute for Ronald as he struggled to understand his father's problem. Here, mystery and doubt abounded—as they often do when people attempt to make sense out of life and death issues. But as Ronald asked, "Can faith allow me to live with myself, and for the sake of Christ and my people, without certainty? Without doubt? Can I live faithfully where there are signs in my ministry that read, 'No answer'? Is genuine faith possible without confusion over things that matter to us in life?" Questions of this sort are apparently always there in the shadows of our ministries of outreach and concern in human community. They are ever-present in the faith pilgrimage and life story of Ronald Packnett, as he seeks to respond to the demands of the gospel in the world. At the close of our interview and conversation, I left with the feeling that what may, indeed, command increasing attention in his own ministry would be the struggle of how to celebrate—in the freedom of the spirit—the meaning of faith without having all the answers.

DISCUSSION NOTES

Being black in the South during the mid-1950s and early 1960s was not easy. The external symbols of the "old South" were everywhere, from racially segregated schools and restaurants to public toilets and white water fountains. But there are also many chilling accounts of blacks who migrated from the South to the North in search of the American dream and were cruelly greeted with a welcome mat that read, "Niggers, stay in your place!" Ironically, parts of the North—such as Chicago's South Side—were not much different from the country hamlets and cotton fields of the old South.

Ronald Packnett was an exceptional black youth growing up on the South Side of Chicago: He exercised the gift of self-determination. He beat the odds. Given the demoralizing boundary of black ghetto life in urban America, Ronald turned that negative into a positive. For many black ghetto youths, however, the threatening thunder of the "negative" in urban life drowns out the tamed echo of the "positive." In this case, there are at least three related issues that may evoke discussion and critical reflection in the Christian community. The first one is the influence of Grandma Ella on Ronald's life and spiritual formation. Throughout our discussion, Ronald spoke candidly and appreciatively of her moral and spiritual values.

The second issue is the theological issue of the perception of God in the black experience in America. Even as a minister, Ronald's perception of the gospel seems to have been shaped by his grandmother's view that God must be first in our lives. For discussion, we may ask, for example, What can we learn about God from Grandma's use of religious language?

The third issue in this case that may trigger valuable discussion and insight is Ronald's relationship to his father, Nicholas Broadnax. He describes the troubled relationship as a love-hate affair, burdened with obvious pain, compassion, and guilt. How do we see the compassionate face of God in a torn and shattered relationship between a father and son? What sort of values should a Christian live by? These are important questions and concerns for interpersonal or group dialogue. Some Christians may find useful William A. Jones, Jr.'s volume, *God in the Ghetto*.

Ethical Approach

1. Are there parallels between Ronald's life story and faith and your own?
2. What stories or sayings do you recall from your childhood that shaped your life?
3. From your own moral or theological perspective, how would you assess the phrase, "If the Lord willing"?

Issues for Reflection

1. What do you make of Grandma Ella's emphasis on moral discipline and respect for Jim Crow customs?
2. Sketch out a plan for better understanding Ronald's relationship to his father? Is it an ideal plan?
3. What roles should families play in shaping our God-concepts, in the light of human oppression?

SUGGESTED READING

Chesnutt, Charles W. *The Marrow of Tradition*. Ann Arbor: University of Michigan Press, 1967.

Cone, James H. *The Spirituals and the Blues*. New York: Seabury Press, 1972.

DuBois, W.E.B. *The Souls of Black Folk*. New York: Fawcett Publications, 1961.

Jones, William A., Jr. *God in the Ghetto*. Elgin, Ill.: Progressive Baptist Publishing House, 1979.

Kunjufu, Jawanza. *Countering the Conspiracy to Destroy Black Boys*. Chicago: Afro-Am Publishing Co., 1984.

Rose, Arnold. *The Negro in America*. New York: Harper & Row, 1964.

Staples, Robert. *Black Masculinity*. San Francisco: Black Scholar Press, 1982.

Thurman, Howard. *The Luminous Darkness*. New York: Harper & Row, 1965.

Wyne, Marvin D., Kinnard P. White, and Richard H. Coop. *The Black Self*. Englewood Cliffs, N.J.: Prentice-Hall, 1974.

Wynn, Daniel W. *The Black Protest Movement*. New York: Philosophical Library, 1974.

CASE
16

LINE UP!
LINE UP!

"More than ten years have come and gone since I finished college, but I still can hear my mother's sassy, commanding voice echoing in my ears: 'Line up! Line up!' " These words fell from the lips of Gloria Y. Perkins as she reflected on the life and fruitful struggles of her mother who had recently retired from her career as a public school teacher in Carbondale, Illinois, after more than a quarter of a century of service. Musing on her childhood, Gloria fondly recalled, "I can remember as a child being taken by my mother to church school, along with friends . . . We all had a good time there, but in the midst of all the gala singing, shouting, praying, and testifying, my mother never failed to say to us, 'Get in line.' This was her code for alerting us to the value of education as a tool to success and well-being as black Americans . . . You see, children in the community got a double-dose of mama because she taught in both public school and Sunday school."

But the matter under consideration in this case is not the life experiences and musings of a daughter named Gloria, but those of her mother, Geraldine Browning Perkins, who has both a deep love for children and a passionate thirst for education. Geraldine Browning was born October 6, 1918, in the small, rural, prairie town of Metropolis, in southern Illinois; she was born to Viola and Henry Browning. Her father, Henry Browning, was a farmer who diligently worked about eighty acres of land that often produced barely enough food and grain to sustain a growing family. But proud, stoic, and stern, and with striking features, Papa Browning had a love for the rich soil. In the mid-1920s and early 1930s, rural life was hard for black people, and Papa Browning earned less than two dollars per day for his labor and grain. Yet on this wage he took care of a wife, maintained a household, and eventually educated Geraldine, his only daughter.

It has been said the journey of faith is like a branch of a wildflower, which runs in many directions. Such a branch grew strong in the Browning family's adherence to the "Protestant work ethic." One may say in the idiom of Geraldine's cultural heritage that such a value-orientation can be referred to as a Nubian work ethic. Here the notion of a Nubian work ethic is characterized, in part, by such moral values as frugality, integrity, self-initiative, beneficence, and social solidarity in one's struggle to achieve certain goals in life. The term "Nubian" is used to imply black heritage and tradition. This work ethic found vigorous expression in this family; Geraldine's father believed that "for every two pennies earned, one must be saved."

This practical philosophy enabled him eventually to build his own house with his own hands and to win the respect of his neighbors in Massac County. Young Geraldine was noted for her energy and buoyant spirit around the farm. The family raised many farm products for consumption in the local market, including corn, beans, wheat, and potatoes. Because of her assertiveness and outgoing personality, Geraldine soon developed a reputation around the county as being able to handle a "mule and plow as good as any man!" Her strength of body was matched by strength of mind, and she graduated in 1937 as valedictorian of her class at the Karnak Community High School.

With a natural love for the soil and farm life, Geraldine initially decided to study agriculture but was convinced by Etta W. Jackson, a remarkable Christian woman and teacher, that elementary education and the training of young people were her true calling and passion as a servant of God. Mom Jackson, as Etta was affectionately called by community folk, had been a well-respected teacher at the high school in Carbondale, Illinois, for many years. Her demeanor and her work as a teacher and a woman of faith helped to create civic awareness of the need for education among black children and the disadvantaged, in general. Once Geraldine had decided on a career in education, there was no turning her away from implementing the promise education held for black progress and freedom.

In the traditional black community, the Bible was the primer, the first book of great literature that black people learned to read. Why? The Bible was regarded as the "Good Book" that allowed blacks to feel that they were "somebody in a land that treated them like a nobody!" Therefore, the Bible played a crucial role in the formation of Geraldine's self-understanding. As a child, she "read" the Bible largely through the eyes of her grandfather. Grandpa Bridges instilled in her four basic moral and religious values. "I'll never forget the kind of thing papa would talk about in our household," remembered Geraldine. "The first thing was reverence for God, in good times as well as bad times . . . The 'name' was taken seriously." Geraldine recalled, for instance, that whenever a special program or cultural event was held at the church, no public speaker would dare begin without prefacing his or her address with the phrase, "Giving honor and glory to God."

A second value Geraldine learned by family example is expressed in the phrase "line up," which signified for her not only the agrarian ethic of hard work as the way to achievement and well-being, but also an approach to religion. The words actually held many shades of meaning which included, "line up with the church," "line up with God," "line up with the right vocation," "line up with the right spouse," "line up with right-thinking people in community."

Equally important in shaping Geraldine's values was the emphasis in the Browning family on avoiding bad company. Said Geraldine, "We were taught by our folks not to be 'spotted by the world.' " This meant among other things that people of faith and Christian character in the black community must be especially mindful not to hang out in so-called red light districts or up on the levee, where "gamblers, dancers, backsliders, and sinners abounded. Grandpa Bridges felt that these sort of people were on the fast track and didn't mean anybody no good in the community," quipped Geraldine. Geraldine paused for a minute. Her mind suddenly flashed to the book of Psalms, and she softly spoke these familiar words:

Blessed is the man
who walks not in the counsel of the wicked,
nor stands in the way of sinners,
nor sits in the seat of scoffers.
                    (Psalm 1:1)

I found it interesting that the Bible was always displayed in a prominent spot in the Browning house; usually it was placed in the back bedroom on the old wooden dresser which was neatly laced in white linen. Raised in the Church of Christ, Geraldine frequently turned to the Bible for guidance and strength. Grandpa Bridges also taught her that she need not try to bear her burdens alone. "Where there is a problem or trial, just take it to the Lord," he would often say.

Perhaps the most important value that Geraldine picked up from the example of her elders was what she called "clean living." As a Christian, she believed this value was most crucial for raising a family.

And, indeed, the joys and problems of family life did not elude her. In 1939, Geraldine met and fell in love with William C. Perkins, and they were soon married. They have two daughters, Delores and Gloria, and a son, William Jr. Concerning the family values that shaped her own identity and faith pilgrimage, Geraldine Perkins cheerfully remarked, "The life I live is the best teacher of values in the family . . . Though it isn't always easy, you should try to finish what you start, if you can and if it's a good thing. This is why I tell all my children to line up!"

Geraldine's testimony about the importance of faith and family values in shaping identity is demonstrated in her role as an educator in the community. In a culture in which black children felt the sting of discrimination and the constant burden of poverty, Geraldine's colleagues say, "She opened up a new world to disadvantaged children through education and her positive philosophy of self-belief." She taught her own children that it is what is on the "inside" that really counts; that skin color or blackness is a burden "only to those who allow it to be." In short, she impressed upon all the children she taught that a person acquires a sense of selfhood and freedom through faith in God and belief in their ability. As a testament to their mother's beliefs and practices, Delores, Gloria, and William all became committed teachers in the tradition of their mother!

By now our conversation was near its end, but it could not conclude without my posing a few questions regarding the future of black youths in our society. I asked Geraldine three questions: What problems do our young people face today? What has gone wrong? How do you see young people in light of your own values and faith story? Until now, Geraldine had sat quietly at the kitchen table. But now she stood up and paced the floor in a moment of solitude. Then she began to speak. "As early as I can remember, even as a child, I was taught by my folks never to be a quitter, never to give up when faced with a problem or crisis . . . Believe me, I had my share of hurts and disappointments growing up as a country girl. You know, I can remember that some of my in-laws and neighbors felt that I shouldn't try to go to college while trying to help raise my family at the same time . . . But that was *their* judgment and not mine. My papa used to say to me, 'Take every man's censure, but reserve your own judgment.' I feel strongly that today many of our young people lack the parental guidance that we took for granted then."

Again I asked, "What has gone wrong?" Geraldine stopped pacing and quietly took a seat at the opposite end of the kitchen table. A look of solemn intensity came over her face as she turned the question over in her mind. "Maybe we all are to blame to some extent; maybe our whole society has let our young people down by giving them so many mixed signals . . . But I also feel that many young people today, in our own community, want success without paying a price; they want opportunity to just fall from the sky into their laps—with little effort on their part. I still feel somehow that you must prepare yourself as a young person *before* the 'door opens'—not *when* the door opens. I do believe in the promise of our youths; this is the reason I go back to my faith to 'line up,' though we don't really know what's behind the door. But today, I'm not sure that our young people understand this simple truth that well, and I really worry at this point."

There is always a mix of anguish and joy, dread and hope in sharing one's own story as an affirmation of faith. What determines whether our faith grows or withers away like a frost-bitten flower of the field may depend on how we see and communicate what we experience, as we line up before the presence of God.

DISCUSSION NOTES

There are amazing parallels between the faith stories and struggles of Africans from the so-called old country and African-Americans. The Christian values of the black experience—whether in Africa or America—echo the sounds of faith, struggle, courage, hard work, and a tough-minded love determined to make the world a better place to live. For Geraldine Perkins, being raised in a small midwestern prairie town where such values as community and hard work were emphasized actually seemed to enhance her moral view that education opens a window to the world. There is an old African adage that expresses this socio-cultural sentiment well: "The blood that unites us as an African people is thicker than the ocean that divides us."

Some of the pertinent issues for discussion in this case are:
1. The mother-daughter relationship in African-American culture, especially as it is imaged through Gloria's deep affection and respect for her mother, Geraldine.
2. The appreciation of the value of hard work in the home as a precondition to educational achievement and character formation. Some may see this part of the "Nubian work ethic" as an African-American counterpart to the so-called Protestant work ethic. It is

symbolized in Geraldine's orders to the children to "line up!" or "get in line!"

3. The crucial theological concern for "reverence for God" in all seasons of human life.

Here it may be well to point out that for Geraldine, in particular, and the black community in general, the trials and tribulations of growing up black in America have always been eased by two things—education and a strong faith in the God of the Bible—both of which will see you through the storms of life. In the faith tradition of the black church, there is a powerful line from an old gospel song that reads,

Oh Lord, when the storms of life are raging stand by me;
When the world is tossing me like a ship out on the seas,
Thou who rules wind and water stand by me!

Hence, the shaping values of reverence for God and education informed Geraldine's self-understanding as a Christian believer and public school teacher. In discussing this case, the reader may be challenged to consider the crucial issues of education in contemporary society and the sort of moral commitment needed in order to make a positive difference in the lives of others. Undoubtedly, reflection on the issues may also distress us as we ponder the seeming lack of positive black role models in our society today.

Ethical Approach

1. As a person of faith, what is your ethical response to the words "line up"?
2. Are these words more likely to have more meaning for some people?
3. What might the words "line up" suggest to us about the value of discipline in the home or school?

Issues for Reflection

1. How would you assess Geraldine Perkins's emphasis on the role of traditional family values in building a foundation for success among youths today?
2. Beyond an education, what do teachers owe students?
3. Through our own faith stories, how can we better equip young people for the future?

SUGGESTED READING

Afrik, Hannibal. *Education for Self-Reliance*. Stanford, Calif.: Council of Independent Black Institutions, 1981.

Fleming, Jacquelyn. *Blacks in College*. San Francisco: Jossey-Bass, 1985.

Franklin, V. P. *Black Self-Determination: A Cultural History of the Faith of the Fathers*. Westport, Conn.: Lawrence Hill & Co., 1984.

Gardner, Howard. *Frames of Mind: The Theory of Multiple Intelligences*. New York: Basic Books, 1983.

Goodlad, John. *A Place Called School*. New York: McGraw-Hill, 1984.

Hale-Benson, Janice E. *Black Children: Their Roots, Culture, and Learning Styles*. Baltimore: Johns Hopkins University Press, 1986.

Kunjufu, Jawanza. *Countering the Conspiracy to Destroy Black Boys*. Chicago: Afro-Am Publishing Co., 1982.

———. *Developing Positive Self-Images and Discipline in Black Children*. Chicago: African-American Images, 1984.

Thurman, Howard. *The Centering Moment*. San Francisco: Friends United, 1980.

Webber, Thomas C. *Deep Like the Rivers*. New York: W. W. Norton & Co., 1978.

Wilson, Amos. *The Developmental Psychology of the Black Child*. New York: Africana Research Publishing, 1978.

17

DRINKING AND THEOLOGY
DON'T MIX

Aaron Jackson is forty-two, a gray-haired man of slender build. He lives in St. Louis and has never married. The eldest son of Henry Jackson and Judith Harris, he has four sisters and six brothers. While his family is a sprawling mix of Baptists, Pentecostals, and Presbyterians, its religious roots lie in the Christian Methodist Episcopal (CME) church.

Dissatisfied with his career as a teacher, Aaron recently decided to pursue the vocation of Christian ministry. Before teaching, he had worked parttime in public transportation for ten years, so ministry would be his third career. While not totally convinced that it was the right career choice for him, for better or worse he appeared to be driven by an inner force to give it a try.

Aaron enrolled at Walker Theological Seminary. Walker was established less than a decade ago in answer to the need for advanced lay training in theology and evangelism. The school is theologically and socially conservative in matters of sex, morality, marriage and family life, religion, and politics. Activities such as drinking and smoking are frowned upon. This theological community tends to interpret Christian tradition and doctrine from a highly conservative and fundamentalist perspective, and regards liberalism and humanism as enemies of the divine truth as revealed in holy scripture.

Aaron's first year of academic study was extremely difficult. He often complained about the workload, the frequent exams, and the seemingly endless reading requirements. He confessed to a friend that year, ''To be honest, I barely made it through my foundational courses . . . I felt like giving up many times and going back into teaching, but I stuck it out.'' After much toil and personal struggle, Aaron finished his first year. But that was only the beginning of what became a slowly growing personal nightmare.

In his second year in seminary, for reasons he does not fully understand, Aaron lost the discipline needed to study—and at his best, he had been academically marginal. He began to suffer periodic depression, as his feelings of self-doubt and failure grew. In his bewilderment, Aaron began to drink. It would appear that drinking became a way for Aaron to cope with his day-to-day problems on the campus.

One of the school's policies required that individuals must report to the "proper authority" anyone found drinking or violating other rules governing student life. (This strict policy grew, in part, out of a tragic alcohol-related automobile accident involving two Walker students, one of whom died; the other student was permanently injured.) Obviously, Aaron could not hide his drinking problem from Paul, his close friend and roommate. But Paul felt sympathy for Aaron and did not want to report him. Eventually, of course, the decision was taken out of his hands.

Aaron's drinking problem gradually became more serious. During the first semester of his second year in seminary, someone reported him to the administration. Within a few weeks, Aaron's case was brought before the Disciplinary Council, part of the Walker theological community. The council is a seven-member body: three faculty representatives, two administration representatives, and two students. Each member of the Disciplinary Council has equal voting power. The level of collegiality that has existed between the administration and faculty can be characterized as "good," although there has been conflict and tension about seminary policies governing student social life. Students have often felt that their concerns have been ignored by the administration. This history of dispute among the administration, faculty, and student body is the environment within which the charges against Aaron were to be heard by the Disciplinary Council.

As could be expected, sentiment among the seven members varied. Most of the representatives from the administration and faculty favored enforcing the policy against drinking, taking an uncompromising and antagonistic position against Aaron. The student representatives and one faculty member appeared more sympathetic and argued that the council's job was "to show compassion and reasonableness" toward Aaron and his alcohol addiction. The moderator of the Disciplinary Council listened carefully to the arguments and charges of the case, which are briefly sketched below. (I use the terms "antagonist" to refer to the administration–faculty position and "protagonist" to reflect the position of the student body.)

ANTAGONIST: To members of the council, I have looked at the case of Aaron Jackson, and I am reasonably convinced that we have one obligation and one obligation only—to uphold the current policies of this institution. Our policy clearly states that the possession and drinking of any alcoholic beverage on campus is strictly prohibited.

PROTAGONIST: During my two years as a student in this seminary community, I feel that students have not had much to say about policies that gravely effect all of us. Personally, I find this policy offensive to my own conscience . . . I don't remember anyone ever asking students what they thought about this policy before it was put into place.

ANTAGONIST: Perhaps the student representative is forgetting that in this community the administration, faculty, and student body are all bound by the same policy. When I came here three years ago, I found the policy already in place . . . Thus by my coming, I agreed to abide by the policies of the community. There is also an issue here of Christian lifestyle, and I don't think that Mr. Jackson is living up to his end of the bargain . . . I find his drinking unacceptable.

PROTAGONIST: As for Christian lifestyle, I really don't see how any one of us on this council can claim perfection; we all have sinned, as the Beloved apostle Paul said, and have "fallen short." Besides, the issue here is not same legal rule or absolute law but "compassion" as we try to respond to the needs of a hurting brother in our midst. Granted that we in training for ministry and service of God in the world are expected to lead sober lives and practice exemplary conduct, but we must also come to see that ministers are human and make mistakes. As Jesus said to the woman caught in adultery, "he who is without fault let him cast the first stone."

ANTAGONIST: Well, I do not think that we should make excuses or moral justifications for human weaknesses. You seem to miss my point altogether: we do not, I believe, need to be reminded that sin is in the world and that sin is also in us. But we as Christians have a duty to do what is right by Mr. Jackson . . . And I need not remind members of this council that we are not running, in this seminary, an alcohol clinic but a theological program; and as far as Christian character is concerned, I do remember Jesus saying to his followers, "Be ye perfect as your heavenly Father is perfect." And throughout the Bible, we are warned not to indulge in strong drink—for drinking of liquor defies the body which is the temple of the Holy Spirit.

PROTAGONIST: I don't know why you're trying to disguise the real issue in this case by citing scripture! As a council we are not here to debate scripture but to do the compassionate and right thing on behalf of a student with a drinking problem—and I just don't think dismissing him is the right answer. If I may be pardoned for doing myself what I just criticized you for doing, I simply remind the esteemed members of this council that the Bible also teaches us to "love one another," and I cannot see, for the life of me, how dismissing Aaron is a loving or responsible act on our part.

ANTAGONIST: If we allow Aaron to stay on in this theological community, what will other students think if our policy? Well, I'll tell you how they will probably react: they will lose respect for our authority! If we change the rule for Aaron and his situation, why bother to have a policy or rule in the first place?

PROTAGONIST: Maybe that's the point.

ANTAGONIST: What do you mean?

PROTAGONIST: The policy on drinking is too cut and dry.

ANTAGONIST: Bunk! It has served us well so far as an institution, and I don't see a need for change now.

PROTAGONIST: But we're not simply dealing with an ironclad rule but with the life of a real person and with his future.

ANTAGONIST: Well, we didn't make the policy, but we *are* obligated to uphold it and to safeguard the moral standards of this community. After all, when will students ever learn that theology and drinking don't mix!

PROTAGONIST: Members of the council, we need to consider how our decision will affect Aaron's life and ministry, and not just be concerned about rules and regulations set up by this institution. There is a lot at stake here in terms of our faithfulness.

MODERATOR: Perhaps we have heard enough from both sides regarding the dilemma and drinking problem of Aaron Jackson. Whatever else may be said or done, we are obligated as a council to vote our consciences.

After lengthy and agonizing debate over the problems and concerns presented in the case of Aaron Jackson, the Disciplinary Council voted four to three to dismiss him from Walker Theological Seminary.

DISCUSSION NOTES

This particular case may give us a valuable point of departure in discussing an issue that makes, I think, most liberal Christians feel a bit uneasy—social drinking. The case is about Aaron Jackson, a second-year seminarian, who finds himself at odds with the on-campus policy that prohibits the use of alcoholic beverages on campus. It seems to me that liberal Western Protestant theology tends to look the other way when attempts are made to address the complex problem of social drinking. Inadvertently or intentionally, many liberal Christians seem to dismiss the issue and pretend that it is a primarily a matter of personal morality.

It is argued by many, including liberal, mainline Protestants that social drinking is a matter of moral choice and that tolerance to alcohol cannot be legislated. After all, they argue, if a person can "hold his liquor," why should others care so long as he doesn't hurt anybody. Such an argument is often made by ordinary, decent people who feel obligated to uphold the principles of tolerance and pluralism, which tend to be reduced to the glib slogan, "You do your thing; I'll do mine—and if, by chance, we meet that's beautiful!"

However, this case also raises the wider issue of freedom versus authority: How do we reconcile the claims of individual freedom and conscience with the authority of an institution to uphold its social policy? Some attention, in regular group discussion, may be given to this wider issue of the case.

In dialogue, readers may also want to discuss the social issue of why people turn to alcohol in the first place. Of course, I suspect that to raise the question implies prior internal agonizing and moral deliberation. A cursory list of reasons why people drink may include loneliness, the need for attention and acceptance, escapism, peer pressure, rebellion against prescribed norms, curiosity, chilling-out, ego reinforcement, self-aggran-dizement, boredom, spiritual numbness; the list goes on.

In any event, the point to be made in this case is that the problem of drinking is more complex than what we first assume. We can turn to scripture for moral injunctions about drinking. In light of the moral dilemmas of this case, individuals or discussion groups may wish to read and ponder Deut. 21:20; Isa. 29:9; Matt. 11:19; Eph. 5:18; 1 Cor. 5:11; 1 Tim. 3:3; and Tit. 1:7. The material presented in this case also presumes that drinking per se, is not an isolated problem—the effect is always on individual persons, families, and communities which are integral to the common good. To comprehend the kinds of effects drinking can have on behavior—regardless of one's liberal or conservative views—we must be intentional in our efforts to learn more about the problem in the wider society. Here I am not trying to uphold the virtues or to critique, in a moralistic way, the vices of drinking but rather to point to the need for continuing reflection on the issue itself. Perhaps the bottom line is commitment to moral deliberation, since the potential for alcohol abuse is high in our culture.

Ethical Approach

1. What biblical resources would you draw upon to respond to Aaron's dilemma?
2. As a friend or counselor, what would be your approach to a person with a drinking problem?
3. Are there nonbiblical resources that can be useful? If so, what are they?

Issues for Reflection

1. What are the issues that claim your attention in this case?
2. In what ways do you agree with the decision made by the Disciplinary Council?
3. In what ways do you disagree?

SUGGESTED READING

Adams, Jay E. *The Christian Counselor's Casebook*. Grand Rapids: Baker Book House, 1974.

Ferm, Deane William, ed., *Liberation Theology North American Style*. New York: International Religious Foundation, 1987.

Lewis, G. Douglass. *Resolving Church Conflict: A Case Study Approach for Local Congregations*. New York: Harper & Row, 1981.

McCall, Emmanuel L. *Black Church Lifestyles*. Nashville: Broadman Press, 1986.

McCarthy, Donald G., and Edward J. Bayer, eds. *Handbook on Critical Life Issues*. St. Louis, Mo.: Pope John Center, 1982.

Miller, Haskell M. *Who Sets the Standards? Behavior, Society and the Church*. New York: Pilgrim Press, 1989.

Neal, Marie Augusta. *A Socio-Theology of Letting Go*. New York: Paulist Press, 1977.

Nolan, Richard T., et al. *Living Issues in Ethics*. Belmont, Calif.: Wadsworth Publishing Co., 1982.

Ray, Oakley S. *Drugs, Society, and Human Behavior*. St. Louis, Mo.: C. V. Mosby Co., 1972.

Sider, Ronald J., ed. *Lifestyle in the Eighties*. Philadelphia: Westminster Press, 1982.

Weeks, Louis B. *Making Ethical Decisions*. Philadelphia: Westminster Press, 1987.

18

A VIEW FROM
THE BOTTOM

"Maybe what I did in 1968 was leading to what I am now. Man, I was sick and tired of what I was doing—and I stood up for my manhood," said Vernon Eversley, a forty-year-old college graduate from New York City. The social prism through which we must look at this case is the "street corner society" that at one time satisfied the cravings and desires of Vernon's troubled life. There was, of course, much to be troubled about in 1968, as political, economic, and moral forces converged to demand radical national social change. It was not just the war protestors, the civil rights marchers, the black militants, the hippies and yippies who echoed the need for change, but the voiceless victims of drugs and despair who aimlessly walked city streets and slept in the alleys of urban decay. Vernon Eversley is the sort of person who knows well the burden of victimization so often depicted in modern black literature. Personal testimony of faith and struggle tends to be partial to irony and surprise. One of the surprises in Vernon Eversley's life story is that he beat the odds—the tragic social odds of growing up poor and black in Harlem and of dying young and nameless.

Vernon Eversley knows well the drug scene of Harlem—its glorious deceptions, greed, violence, and its seduction of the human spirit. He knows well this "culture-within-a-culture," where the prevailing social norms of the Anglo-Saxon community are out of sync with the rhythm of black ghetto life. The victims of Vernon's world—quietly disguised as they were by a history of neglect, pain, and abuse—did not proudly wear a symbolic cross around their necks, but bands around their drug-worn arms that told the story of a thousand needle pricks. The patron saints of Vernon's world required not the faith of a "mustard seed," but the sniffing of a paregoric seed; they required followers to show not hospitality but hostility to the outsider, not unconditional love where despair gives way to hope but unabridged lust where death stalks its prey in the dark of the night. From 1968 to 1980, Vernon's life moved in response to the twisted values and sounds of this social world. But somehow, miraculously, he found the inner strength to break free from the drug world and its idolatrous aberrations and lustful glitter.

Vernon's pilgrimage and struggle is really a story of many beginnings and detours. A friendly but cautious man, Vernon was born in Georgetown, Guyana, in Central America. His father, John Eversley, was a merchant seaman, and his mother, Beryl, was a devoted and faithful housewife. Raised in a strict Anglican family, young Vernon found his family's rules and social values to be too authoritarian and repressive. Many times in his youth he ran away from home for long periods. Usually, he would stay with close friends, although he did have an older brother, Cecil, to whom he felt close, as well as a younger brother and sister. As time passed, Vernon found himself drawn more and more to the seductive glamour and pleasures of street life. He became part of the criminal subculture, including gang fights, and petty crime. At the age of fourteen, he left his home in Guyana in the hope of finding a better way of life in New York City. But with little money and no job, Vernon soon found that life there was not as sweet as he had been led to believe.

In fact, life in Harlem was tough. Of course, Vernon had a few friends who had come to America earlier, and he stayed with them for awhile. But what he saw at first glance in the ghetto was hopelessness and fear, despite the storefront churches that dotted the crowded streets of Harlem. Vernon spoke of his feelings about life in Harlem, then and now: "A lot of people in the streets here have given up . . . They see the world as out of their control, and they say, 'What's the use? Why struggle since things ain't getting any better? What's the use of trying? Even the people, man, in the so-called system are not really free. They, too, will take you for a bad ride. So why bother?' "

Suspicious, fearful, and cautious in this strange new land called America, Vernon Eversley increasingly found himself drifting and being pulled by both sides of his being. Like many Americans who have a cultural heritage despised by some and grudgingly admired by others, Vernon had a desire to prove himself and to make good in this new land. But that dream would be difficult to fulfill. He quickly discovered that in Harlem you never deal from a deck where the face cards are honestly marked, that is, you never live by the fruits of the Spirit, with love, kindness, and mercy. Instead, the masterdealer of the streets takes the shortcuts of deceit, greed, and self-advantage, and the law of the jungle reigns.

Led in part by his thirst for both freedom and self-improvement, Vernon had faith in faith; he somehow believed that he could survive the madness and craziness of Harlem street life. During his most trying years in the ghetto, he admitted to me, his inner strength undoubtedly came from his mother's faith. He had never fancied himself to be a religious person in a formal sense, although he had believed in the power of God in human affairs. But as we got deeper into our conversation about his pilgrimage, I asked Vernon, "What does faith mean when your back is against the wall in the ghetto?" He replied, "I think it's real nice to have faith in God, though I don't know what all that might mean for the life I live . . . Faith might mean that God takes care of street people and fools; I was both because I did what I had to do to survive. I stayed on rooftops and basements, in jails with drunks, drug users, and prostitutes; at least in jail I was warm and got soup and crackers to chase away my hunger pains . . . If faith is surviving, then I must have it."

But the reality in Vernon's personal story was not faith in the sense in which we ordinarily recognize it. Indeed, Vernon was quick to point out to me that he did not have faith in the sense of being a confessing Christian, a Muslim, a Hindu, or a Jew. In fact, there was nothing in his personal testimony or life story which suggested a ritual of adherence to some formal doctrine or dogma. To the contrary, I observed that his was a sort of "faith qua faith," a dogged determination to survive the madness of the ghetto; he was motivated by the fear and death that awaited Vernon Eversley around every dark corner.

The transition from the painful struggles of the dark ghetto to college life was not easy. But somehow Vernon found inner strength in the sudden recognition that the goal of college was beyond neither his reach nor his mental capability. It was as if Vernon reasoned within himself— to use an idiom popularized in the black church tradition—that "a man's reach must exceed his grasp or what's a heaven for." In 1980, Vernon Eversley enrolled at St. Cloud State University and, through self-discipline and hard work, graduated five years later with a B.A. in philosophy and political science. Vernon is still surprised over his success and the turnaround in his life. As we talked further, it was hard for him to identify exactly the starting point of his "new beginning," his move away from the seduction and pestilence of the drug scene. Like a convert fresh from the wilderness of sin, all Vernon knew was that a change had taken place! Something had happened. He had escaped. Vernon's struggle and rendez-vous with the drug culture was now a closed chapter of his personal history.

It is interesting to note that since college, Vernon has devoted himself to improving black life in Harlem. His particular moral concern now is the development of community-based programs to combat what he called "the unfinished business of racism and sexist oppression that pollute whole communities and churches in our society." One of the things that bothers him about Christianity, for instance, is not that it is the "white man's religion," as some blacks charge, but that in our society it has become a religion devoid of the compassionate teachings of Jesus, who cast his lot with the outcasts and the poor. Reflecting on how things might be different for street people in the future, especially in terms of faith, Vernon exclaimed, "The people I know from the world I came from are down and lowly; they're folks who have been excluded and counted out by society. But I have a strange faith that things can be different for them and us . . . Yet, sadly, it's not the kind of faith I see on display either in the black church or, even less, in the mainstream church."

Apparently many of these folks did not fully understand that Vernon's struggle against the social forces of his world was—deep, deep down—a human cry for justice and self-acceptance. It bothers him that there appears to be little genuine acceptance of his views by that wider society. He feels also that church people in the black community have failed to identify with the nameless and faceless masses at the bottom of society. "They're too busy with status symbols and big cars," he said, adding that he is both saddened and disturbed that so few churches in the ghetto see the homeless problem as one of "faithfulness" to the Jesus they sing about and pray to each Sunday morning. "Although I am not a Chris-tian," explained Vernon, "I do know that Jesus Christ told his disciples to feed the hungry and clothe the naked—in other words, to be concerned about street people, about people who have been on the bottom like me."

As one whose life has been touched by the power of the Christian faith, I must admit that I was disturbed and embarrassed to hear such criticism of the black Christian community. For so much of what Vernon expressed is painfully real. I could see moral indignation and rage on Vernon's face as we moved toward the end of our conversation.

Vernon's long-range plans are not clear; despite his moral outrage, he seems to be joyously grateful for the gift of daily life. However, what is clear to Vernon and what his heart knows is that "street life" gives a person a view from the bottom that should scandalize the people at the top who hold the power. To be sure, Vernon Eversley has made one giant stride away from the culture of the streets, but many more strides still remain to be taken.

DISCUSSION NOTES

This case study is interesting and provocative because Vernon Eversley's story is also the story of one of the most morally difficult but hopeful periods in American history. The 1960s was a time of extraordinary social change and racial tension. On the one hand, it was a period marked by a "revolution of rising expectations." On the other hand, it was a period in our collective social life marred by racial bigotry, violence, rage, and a deep sense of powerlessness on the part of African-Americans. Martin Luther King, Jr., eloquently described this racially troubled period as a perilous encounter between whites and blacks who were symbols for the battle of "immoral power versus powerless morality." This is, I believe, the real sociocultural backdrop for grappling with the critical issues in Vernon's case.

While many important issues are raised in this case, I was especially struck by Vernon's concern for self-improvement and a better way of life. For Vernon, the hope for a better life meant leaving his home in Georgetown, Guyana, for the urban sounds and glitter of New York City. His early dreams of self-improvement personally and socially ran up against the harsh realities of drugs, violence, and despair that, except for God's saving grace and the legacy of his mother's faith, almost engulfed Vernon's life. As the data suggests, Vernon's social reality was made up largely of drug users, prostitutes, and the homeless, who were condemned to a life of poverty and shame in the streets of Harlem. The twin themes of survival and black rage seem to permeate this case and tell us something about Vernon Eversley's unique struggles and moral character.

The wider Christian community may logically ask, What functional use can this case story provide? Regular discussion and ethico-theological reflection may move in several directions and may help us to (1) clarify our values and current attitudes toward racism and social injustice in today's society; (2) discuss the particular problem of drug abuse among youths and adults; and (3) discuss Vernon's inner struggle to survive the madness of ghetto life, a struggle that we see as a "profile in courage." Group discussion, therefore, may evoke mixed feelings and expressions of both hope and moral rage as churches struggle with their own sense of mission and calling to the poor and homeless in urban America. In this

regard, discussion leaders and students may find helpful Wolfgang Stegemann's volume, *The Gospel and the Poor,* and Orlando Costas's book,
The Integrity of Mission: The Inner Life and Outreach of the Church. In
discerning the ethical task in the local church, these volumes are highly
recommended for group discussion and interpersonal sharing.

Ethical Approach

1. What should be the responsibility of the black church in response to
the growing number of street people in our society?
2. What procedure or strategy do we follow to make real the biblical
mandate to "feed the hungry and clothe the naked"?
3. How do we choose among those in great need, given the limitation
of current resources?

Issues for Reflection

1. In what ways can you identify with the problems and dilemmas of
Vernon Eversley?
2. Is Vernon's criticism of the black church in the community justified?
3. Describe your own understanding of faith and how it may differ
from Vernon's.
4. How can the church enable victims and the hurting ones in human
society to better distinguish between their basic needs and their
desires?

SUGGESTED READING

Cone, James H. *Black Theology and Black Power.* New York: Lippincott, 1969.
———. *Speaking the Truth.* Grand Rapids: Wm. B. Eerdmans, 1986.
Costas, Orlando. *The Integrity of Mission.* New York: Harper & Row, 1979.
Frazier, E. Franklin. *The Negro Church in America.* New York: Schocken Books,
1969.
Harding, Vincent. *There Is a River.* New York: Harcourt Brace Jovanovich, 1981.
Lenwand, Gerald, ed. *The Negro and the City.* New York: Washington Square
Press, 1968.
Madhubuti, Haki R. *Black Men: Obsolete, Single, Dangerous?* Chicago: Third
World Press, 1990.
Plumpp, Sterling. *Black Rituals.* Chicago: Third World Press, 1976.
Stegemann, Wolfgang. *The Gospel and the Poor.* Philadelphia: Fortress Press,
1984.
Thomas, Latta. *Biblical Faith and the Black American.* Valley Forge, Penna.:
Judson Press, 1976.
Wilmore, Gayraud S. *Black Religion and Black Radicalism.* New York: Double-
day & Co., 1973.

19

THE HIDDEN
RADIANCE

"I never knew my real mother, and my classmates often teased me about that to the point of shame and tears," confessed Veessa Hammond. "But through it all I've learned how to trust in God to supply my every need." This story concerns the hardships and struggles of Veessa Hammond, a Southern black woman, who was born on May 6, 1911. For women of her generation, the story of Mama Veessa, as she was affectionately called by friends, is not unique. What is unique are the incredible and different ways in which ordinary people respond to extraordinary problems and challenges without losing either their basic sanity or their faith in the goodness and mercy of God.

Veessa Hammond grew up in the small town of Brownsville, Tennessee. Educational requirements of the time usually meant that a black child finished the sixth grade and then was expected to take his or her place in society. For many "colored" children of the pre-Depression era (a strange phrase, since most African-Americans still live in a perpetual state of depression), marriage and the responsibilities of family life came quite early, and it was not uncommon for girls of Mama Veessa's generation to marry at fifteen or sixteen. Veessa's education was unusual: she attended Woodstock Preparatory Academy, an old church school in her community. Remember that this was during the early 1920s, when formal education was a rare and scarce commodity for the majority of citizens of African descent.

Leonard Johnson was the headmaster of the school; he was regarded as a fair but strict disciplinarian. There were fifteen fulltime students; Veessa was one of the top pupils in the basic subjects—reading, writing, math, and spelling. Even as a young child, she had an aggressive and outgoing personality and was well-liked by peers and teachers at the academy. She was also respected by people in the broader black community.

Veessa was reared by her Aunt Adda, who was the person who had told Veessa when she was seven of her real mother's death giving birth to her. Aunt Adda was the sort of person who had strength of character, compassion of spirit, seriousness about matters of faith and prayer, and a good sense of humor. For example, on quiet Sunday afternoons, usually between four and seven o'clock, Aunt Adda and many of the children would gather around the fireplace and tell stories of adventure and mystery involving famous people in history. According to Mama Veessa, "Aunt Adda never spent a day in the academy, but knew something about everything . . . She could tell you something funny about anything, from kings and queens of our ancient past all the way down to the vagabonds and poor folks of the present—without missing a thrill or beat. But her favorite book was the Bible, and her favorite story was the tale of Joseph being thrown into the pit by his brothers—but God delivered him from the dark pit."

From the information I gathered in the interview, it was clear that Aunt Adda's was the decisive guiding hand and moral force in rearing young Veessa and giving her a foundation from which to face the storms and challenges of life. Eventually, Veessa finished her formal schooling at the academy and moved to Memphis in search of better employment opportunities. In the 1920s, jobs were very scarce, but Veessa Hammond was determined to survive and eventually managed to find a parttime job at a local dry cleaner. In her struggle to make ends meet, she worked at this job for two years, before leaving to marry Fred Abraham. Youthful and optimistic, Veessa was only sixteen years old and had a lot more growing up to do to cope with big city life. Unfortunately, the marriage itself was short-lived, for her husband suddenly died, leaving her with no means of subsistence. Veessa immediately returned to her childhood community of Brownsville, only to be greeted with the news that her esteemed Aunt Adda had suffered a heart attack. Two weeks later, Aunt Adda also died. These tragic events all took place within a few weeks.

Wounded in spirit but not broken in body, Veessa attempted to pull together a life deeply shattered by the pain of death and personal loss. Now virtually homeless and emotionally restless, Veessa Hammond left her childhood community a second time for Memphis to try "and begin again to mend together my broken life." After several difficult years working at odd jobs, Veessa Hammond met Nathan Jones, a soft-spoken

but persuasive man from Arkansas. A quiet man of character and pru-
dence, Nathan was a carpenter and barber. Between these two individuals, romance grew, and they eventually married. This union proved to
be a happy one which lasted more than thirty-five years. God strength-
ened their hands and hearts by blessing their union with seven children:
Joetta Browning, Mary Gordon, Bud Hammond, Wilma Lambert, White
F. Hammond, Margaret Sidney, and Bertha Stanley. Although they
struggled, Veessa and Nathan had a loving relationship and taught their
children the value of solidarity and of pulling together as a family.

The children were reared in a strongly religious household. Veessa and
Nathan taught the children, by their own example, the importance of
faith in God. Veessa herself was a strong woman of faith and served as
president of the missionary board at the First Baptist Church. Nathan
was also active in church life and community involvement for over forty
years. Together, they taught the children not only to believe in God—in
good times as well as bad—but also to bear witness to the liberating grace
of God in their own life pilgrimages.

I spent many hours in conversation with the children of Mama Veessa
and Nathan. What emerged was a composite of what their parents felt
was important to pass on to the children. Obviously, there were many
experiences worth recalling, but they agreed on four main things. . . .
"Our parents gave us a gift that money can't buy—the inner courage to
speak up for ourselves, and to defend what is right no matter how bad it
hurts . . . Around our old farmhouse mama used to say, 'Every tree must
have its own roots.'

"But that's not all we remember. The value of sharing with the less
fortunate in the community was a 'big thing,' especially for mama. For
instance, we can remember during the beginning of winter—at a time
known by local folks as hog killing season—how mama would often send
nice fresh meat to a close neighbor, Mr. Buddy, who didn't have a family
or much food of his own . . . We didn't understand then as young folks
but we understand now as adults the act of sharing, giving to others who
don't have much never diminishes but enlarges the soul of us all.

"And our home folks, especially mama, taught us the value of risk
taking. She would say that some people try and play it too safe in this
world, and that's no good; . . . it isn't worth the inhibitions it creates.
Her feelings were simply that no gain comes without some risk taking—
remember the turtle; he makes progress only by sticking his neck out.
And the last big thing our parents instilled within us was to 'never get too

big for your own britches.' Always depend on God to lead and guide you in life.''

These were the foundational values that seem to have taken root in the lives of Veessa's adult children. The children were quick to point out that their parents never said that these particular beliefs and values would guarantee smooth sailing, but that they would serve as "anchors" amidst the tempestuous storms of life. Nonetheless, by adopting these family values of hard work, self-reliance, and faith in the God of the Bible, the children grew up to become successful in their own fields. While the family experienced its share of trials and struggles growing up, somehow they found the inner strength to persevere. They found hope in the faith of their mother, who often reminded them of the words of Aunt Adda about confronting the disappointments of life: "There's no need to sit and whine when there's nothing on the line; just bait your hook and keep on trying!''

Instead of allowing her children to feel self-pity or to drown in disappointment, Mama Veessa prodded her children to have courage, to take responsibility for their lives, and to have faith in a God who wills for us "hands of toil" to make human life more human. She taught her children that life's sufferings and toils come to make us strong. What is important, she would say, is to "keep right on trying" and to hold on to your dreams. Mama Veessa shared a story with me regarding the dream of her older son to go to college. There was just one catch: the parents had no money to make that dream come true. At the time, Veessa vividly recalled, financial aid, as such, was very scarce, and only a few high school graduates received college scholarships. Usually, scholarships went to the sons and daughters of principles and teachers in the black community. One day, Veessa had her son sit down and write a letter about his "dream" of attending college, and then not mail the actual letter to anyone, but file it in the secret compartment of his own heart. Within two weeks, this same son enrolled in a noted black college, and four years later he graduated with honors. Some folks would call this nothing short of a miracle; but Veessa Hammond referred to it as "seed faith." This elderly woman of soul then looked right into my eyes and asked, "Have you ever planted the seed of faith?" To say the least I was taken by surprise, as Veessa continued to marvel over the mighty hand of God coming to her rescue in a time of crisis and difficulty, a time when no money was available for college. Like manna from heaven, her money was "seed faith." For Veessa, the notion of "seed faith" was better, symbolically, than real money in the bank. Seed faith is unconditional trust in the love of God as revealed in Jesus Christ, the Liberator and Enabler, who will work everything out all right—despite the trials and hardships in the world. Seed faith renews human life even in the midst of deteriorating health and the presence of physical pain.

Veessa Hammond Jones is seventy-five years old. Her second husband is dead, and she herself is in rapidly deteriorating health. Because of her health problems, the family placed her in a nursing home in their community. The adjustment has been difficult for her and the family, and was not helped by the recent exposure of a long-kept secret: her natural mother—who she had been told had died in childbirth—is actually still living. When Veessa's mother gave the child up at birth, Aunt Adda compassionately took her in and reared her. What an outburst of "hidden radiance!" People in the community who knew about the situation suggest that Veessa's natural mother was prevented by her parents from keeping the baby, as well as from marrying the baby's father.

Mama Veessa is understandably ambivalent about this. Although her children are finding ways to cope with the new situation, they are visibly concerned as to how the knowledge might affect their mother's health and spirit. They visit her often and see to it that her health needs are provided for. But they wonder about her spiritual state of mind. As one of them said in frustration, "I can't imagine how mama feels after all these years thinking that her mother was dead, and now having this big surprise dropped in her lap . . . If I suddenly saw a mother that I never had, I don't know really how I would react—laugh or cry. And it hasn't hit me yet that I will soon lay eyes on a grandmother who never was."

Veessa's oldest son, a minister, finds himself desperately trying to reconcile the family's deep ambivalence and conflict; everyone wonders what joys or problems this new situation will bring. This son has been the mediator and peacemaker in the family throughout the years. But now he finds the family in a new situation that is similar to the prodigal son returning home—except in this instance the "prodigal" is a grandmother nobody knew they had. Without a sense of relief, this son keeps turning over in his own mind the disturbing question, How can we welcome home a grandmother who has never been a part of our home? But as the mediator in the family, he would not dare utter such a question out loud.

DISCUSSION NOTES

The problems, difficulties, and incongruities with which people often struggle in life are never easy to resolve. Therefore, certain values and principles are not unimportant in helping us to clarify the critical issues at stake in human community. Each day people make ethical choices about the people they love, their jobs, their family and children, and their faith and church preference—all of which deeply affect how we perceive and experience social reality. From the data of the case, a significant clue to the social reality which shaped the life and faith of Veessa Hammond was never fully revealed.

Veessa Hammond grew up in a small community that knew well the habits and social customs of a segregated society. To some degree, the "Veessa" depicted in this case is a struggling, nomadic child of the pre-Depression era in America, when blacks were viewed as subordinate to whites. The specifics of this case, however, are not about the wider social problem of race in America. Rather, this is a soul-stirring story about a woman of faith who refused to cave in to the hardships and moral ironies of life. Motherless from birth, Veessa found the love and nurture that sustained her in the gentle but firm character of a distant aunt in Browns-ville, Tennessee. The example of their relationship leads to certain questions: What sort of person was Aunt Adda? How would you describe her relationship to and impact on the life of young Veessa? Who, in your own faith pilgrimage, has served as a significant role model? What sort of ethical problems are created when bad things happen to *faithful* people?

Perhaps one of the issues at stake in this case is not the obvious problem of what could be called "identity dislocation" as a result of Mama Veessa's discovery about her real mother, but the biblical ethic of obedience to God despite uncertainty. Veessa Hammond Jones for most of her life believed her mother was dead. What an awesome challenge to genuine faith to discover the truth! A discussion group may choose to look at the case by contrasting what Kosuke Koyama identifies as two distinctive orientations to religion. One is a "happy-ending religion," in which the Christian believer reduces God to a sugar daddy who fulfills every human desire or need and protects people from the dangerous wilderness experiences of life. The other kind of faith faces the struggles of life and, Koyama rightly argues, is that genuine faith that requires the Christian to go beyond a religion that is merely a "protection from danger" or "happy ending" religion to one rooted in trust in God. I believe that this case, involving the moral struggles and concerns of Veessa Hammond Jones, can be analyzed and ethically considered in terms of Koyama's theological insight. Given the narrative development and complexity of the case, perhaps the following questions or ethical concerns may engender reflection and discussion on the part of us all.

(See Kosuke Koyama, *Three Mile an Hour God* [Maryknoll, N.Y.: Orbis Books, 1979.])

Ethical Approach

1. What would be a responsible approach to this case?
2. What issues of faith do you see?
3. In what ways can an ethic of faith enable siblings to build bridges of mutual support when a parent is threatened by sickness or death?

Issues for Reflection

1. From the perspective of health care, what would be your concerns about Mama Veessa and her sudden knowledge that her birth mother is still alive?
2. How would you likely respond to the situation as a member of the family?
3. Identify and discuss the mixed feelings people often experience when a parent has to be placed in a nursing home.
4. What is the role of the elder son? Should he feel compelled to always be the mediator?

SUGGESTED READING

Bayles, Michael D. *Professional Ethics*. Belmont, Calif.: Wadsworth Publishing Co., 1981.

Benardin, Joseph. *Consistent Ethic of Life*. Kansas City, Mo.: Sheed & Ward, 1988.

Bok, Sissela. *Secrets: On the Ethics of Concealment and Revelation*. New York: Vintage, 1984.

Bouma, Hessel, et al. *Christian Faith, Health, and Medical Practice*. Grand Rapids: Wm. B. Eerdmans, 1989.

Brody, Howard. *Ethical Decisions in Medicine*. 2d ed. Boston: Little, Brown, & Co., 1981.

Browning, Don S., ed., *Pastoral Theology*. Philadelphia: Fortress Press, 1983.

Connery, John R. "The Quality of Life." *Linacre Quarterly* (February 1986).

Flynn, Eileen P. *Hard Decisions*. Kansas City, Mo.: Sheed & Ward, 1990.

Flynn, Eileen P., and Gloria Blanchfield Thomas. *Living Faith: An Introduction to Theology*. Kansas City, Mo.: Sheed & Ward, 1989.

Paris, John J. "When Burdens of Feeding Outweigh Benefits," *Hastings Center Report* (February 1986).

Thornton, Edward E. *Professional Education for Ministry*. Nashville: Abingdon Press, 1970.

CASE
20
A DARK
SECRET

David Nesbitt has been pastor of St. Luke's United Methodist Church for the past six years. A respected community leader, he is outspoken on controversial issues and moral problems. Forty years of age, he is a graduate of a Chicago seminary. His wife, Edith, 33, is a devoted Christian and the mother of their four children—Janet, 15, Alice, 10, Tony, 7, and Benny, 4.

As both a parent and a church leader, David is deeply concerned about social issues and ways in which the church of Jesus Christ can be more responsible to them. He is also concerned that the church serve as a forum wherein lay people can become better informed about serious issues in the church community. As we talked, I was struck by the sense of commitment with which David and Edith grapple with difficult issues of ministry.

The setting for this case is a counseling situation in which David was involved. As in any such situation, the counselor attempts to listen, to understand, to clarify, and to respond faithfully to the issues at stake. It is my conviction that, while Christian ministry comes in many forms, every form of ministry that seeks to be true to the gospel of Jesus Christ must include the questions of faithfulness and freedom in the course of moral struggle in life. As demonstrated here, this case is no exception.

The case involved a married couple in his church, Mark and Sophia Barrington, whom David described as "average" church goers. Unknown to Sophia, Mark had been talking confidentially to David Nesbitt about a bewildering problem. Usually after prayer meeting on Wednesday evening, he would stay for an hour of counseling. The first meeting was emotion-filled but quite puzzling to David Nesbitt. Mark's tone was one of despair, yet he refused to be specific about his problem, saying, "Pastor Nesbitt, I know you can't help me, but just please listen. I don't know what to do. I have to talk to someone . . . The problem I have is tearing me apart; I feel like the bottom just fell out of my life. I'm really scared and terrified. I don't know which way to turn. I have an awful, dark secret." Mark then proceeded to describe a life of infidelity, deception, and immorality that, he said, "would make Jesse James look like Peter Pan!"

But this was as far as he would go. For several sessions, he continued to remain evasive, openly nervous, and seemingly unable to identify precisely what was bothering him. According to David, this made him suspicious, yet he remained deeply concerned for Mark's well-being. At the same time, David silently pondered some questions: What is really going on with Mark and Sophia? What is behind Mark's words, "I feel like the bottom just fell out of my life?" What shameful memory is he hiding that reluctantly drove him into my office? What has faith in God to do with his personal problem? How do I enter his suffering as the pastor?

As David patiently listened to Mark from week to week, it was difficult for him as a counselor to resist thinking about these questions. Looking back at his theological training, he realized that nothing in seminary had quite prepared him for such a difficult moment in pastoral ministry. He constantly struggled with Mark's evasiveness and passive rage as he talked around his real problem. But the pastor continued to show compassion and patience. I found it interesting to note that in our interview David described Christian counseling as "intimate listening." That is precisely what he did for a number of weeks following prayer meeting. "Intimate listening is a hard but fruitful discipline because it forces me to be vulnerable to my people—to try and hear, touch, and feel their hurts," said David Nesbitt. And it was only after weeks of intimate listening that Mark shared his story.

Who is Mark Barrington? He is a thirty-seven-year-old black waiter who lives in Chicago. Deeply troubled, Mark has had questions about his identity and self-image since he was a young child. He is married to Sophia Hudson, and they are the parents of a son, Lewis, and a daughter, Kaiza. Although Mark attends St. Luke's regularly, he has not had as steady a work record in recent years. Sophia was born and raised in a small rural town in southern Illinois and has found urban life a bit rough. The couple has little potential for economic success since Mark made it no further than the eighth grade, and Sophia finished only the tenth grade, dropping out of school then to have their first child. They have been members of St. Luke's for quite some time, since both of their families grew up in the church fellowship.

The gravity of Mark's problem did not begin to unfold until after the birth of their second child, Kaiza. For many years their marriage was full of happiness, love, and meaning, although they had their share of struggles. But eventually Mark began to cheat on his wife. Everybody seemed to have known about Mark's affair except Sophia. Though Sophia had her moments of suspicion, Mark carefully shielded his infidelity from her. This behavior went on for about a year, and the once passionate romance between Mark and Sophia gradually lost its spark. Their marriage was in trouble and, indeed, now seemed beyond help.

As noted earlier, only after weeks of counseling did Mark finally reveal his secret to his pastor. With a pathetic look of desperation and fear on his face, he reluctantly confided, "Oh pastor, help me, I have AIDS . . . I feel there may not be any hope for me at all; my life is messed up and my family all but destroyed because of this terrible thing. What am I to do? Will God ever forgive me?" Sophia was unaware of Mark's problem, but he was frightened that he might have given her AIDS.

If the proverb "A drowning man clutches at straws" is true, then Mark was, apparently, grasping at everything in his reach. Troublesome were his lingering guilt and his feeling that perhaps even God is without mercy and that he was doomed. At the close of his last session, Mark sadly said, "If there is no forgiveness for my messed-up life, at least I hope for a quick death . . . If I must go, oh God, don't let it be a long night of endless pain."

Alarmed but not spiritually subdued by Mark's lament, Pastor Nesbitt briskly spoke. "No, Mark! That's not quite it . . . I mean that's not the way I see it entirely. For one thing, God is not a punishing judge but a merciful parent. We don't know God's mind, for God works in mysterious ways—although it's hard to testify to that. One thing I do know: God cares. God shows mercy and love for fallen creatures like us."

DISCUSSION NOTES

This case is primarily about the problems and moral dilemmas of a counseling situation involving Mark Barrington, a waiter in Chicago. He and Sophia, his wife, have two children, Lewis and Kaiza. In terms of their opportunities in the job market, both parents, as the data in the case sadly indicates, have limited education and job training. Now, after several attempts by Mark to share his problem, Pastor Nesbitt finally discovers Mark's secret: he has contracted AIDS. It is reasonable to assume that while Mark is concerned about his condition, that is not the only issue of this case. From a micro-ethical perspective, there are also counseling issues having to do with guilt, marital infidelity, deception, rage, and the death-dealing hurt inflicted on Sophia and their children.

Is the AIDS victim ever outside of God's mercy and love? Is AIDS a punishment for wrongdoing? As people begin to struggle honestly with the difficult issue of AIDS, most of us agree that there are no easy answers. The case of Mark and Sophia is but a single example of an alarming moral dilemma that exists not only in Western society but in the world community. As we ponder and study the hard problems and deep ethical concerns of this case, it would be well to remember the sobering words of H. L. Mencken, who once remarked, "For every difficult and complex issue there is always an answer that's simple, easy, and wrong!" Thus, I suspect that regular discussion leaders will want to be clear about their interpretive categories, moral baggage, theological bias, and the conflicting emotions each person brings in dialogue and reflection on the particularities of this case.

A word of caution may also be appropriate before further reflection and moral deliberation upon this case. I do not intend to say that in counseling the interpersonal factor or the tragic pain of AIDS and its devastating effect upon the lives of both Mark and Sophia should somehow be minimized. To do so, in my judgment, would be morally wrong and would obscure the essential facts of the case. But I do suggest that we be attentive to at least three "moral directives" as they bear upon the wider issue of AIDS in society.

1. We must try to grapple, honestly and ethically, with the wider problem of *homophobia* in church and society.

2. Careful consideration and guided discussion can focus attention on the issue of AIDS. Approaching the problem as one of social justice in the community, for example, we may ask, Who decides how and where to treat AIDS patients in the interest of the common good? and What are the levels of accountability for showing compassion and justice for those victimized by AIDS, whether they be individuals or Christian families?

3. Always before us, in church and society are the issues of public safety and the right of people to be educated and informed about agonizing problems such as AIDS.

I also strongly recommend for lay and clergypersons W. J. Smith's recent volume, *AIDS: Living and Dying with Hope—Issues in Pastoral Care.*

Ethical Approach

1. From a biblical perspective, what is a faithful response to Mark?
2. What is the role of a Christian counselor in addressing a controversial issue in the life of a church member? The issue of infidelity?
3. How would you advise Sophia to proceed in the relationship with Mark?
4. What is the pastor's responsibility to Sophia?

Issues for Reflection

1. Would it be more important to stress the medical aspect or the family support aspect of Mark's problem?
2. As a follower of Christ and the love ethic, how would you begin as a friend or counselor?
3. What are the wider concerns or implications for the church family of St. Luke's?

SUGGESTED READING

Batchelor, Edward J., Jr. *Homosexuality and Ethics.* New York: Pilgrim Press, 1980.

Berne, Eric. *Sex in Human Loving.* New York: Simon & Schuster, 1973.

Jones, Clinton R. *Homosexuality and Counseling.* Philadelphia: Fortress Press, 1974.

———. *What About Homosexuality?* New York: Thomas Nelson, 1972.

Kirkpatrick, Bill. *AIDS: A Guide for Caregivers.* New York: Pilgrim Press, 1990.

Mace, David R. *The Christian Response to the Sexual Revolution.* Nashville: Abingdon Press, 1970.

Madaras, Lynda. *Talk to Teens about AIDS.* New York: New Market Press, 1988.

Maslow, Abraham. *Toward a Psychology of Being.* Princeton: Van Nostrand, 1952.

Smith, Archie, Jr. *The Relational Self: Ethics and Therapy from a Black Church Perspective.* Nashville: Abingdon Press, 1982.

Spong, John S. *Living in Sin.* New York: Harper & Row, 1988.

Sunderland, Ronald H., and Earl E. Shelp. *AIDS: Personal Stories in Pastoral Perspective.* New York: Pilgrim Press, 1986.